SUPER CUTE

Meringue Cookies, Macarons and Marshmallows

⇒ 50 Fun Recipes ⇐

for Making Unicorns,
Dinosaurs, Zebras, Monkeys
and More

Amy Chao

creator of Cookingwithamyy

PAGE STREET
PUBLISHING CO.

DEDICATION

TO MY PARENTS: FOR RAISING ME TO BELIEVE THAT
ANYTHING IS POSSIBLE IF YOU SET YOUR MIND TO IT

PAGE STREET
PUBLISHING CO.

Copyright © Amy Chao

First published in 2022 by
Page Street Publishing Co.
27 Congress Street, Suite 1511
Salem, MA 01970
www.pagestreetpublishing.com

Distributed by Macmillan, sales in Canada by The Canadian Manda Group.

26 25 24 23 22   1 2 3 4 5

ISBN-13: 978-1-64567-684-3
ISBN-10: 1-64567-684-6

Library of Congress Control Number: 2022937027

Cover and book design by Rosie Stewart for Page Street Publishing Co.
Photography by Wing Lun Fung

Printed and bound in the United States of America

CONTENTS

INTRODUCTION

The art of making meringue cookies, macarons and marshmallows is often underestimated. Using basic ingredients but turning them into anything you like is what makes these treats so versatile and special. Creating specific characters or animals makes them even more special and meaningful when you give them to loved ones.

If you're familiar with my TikTok and Instagram accounts, Cookingwithamyy, then you know all about my signature meringue cookies, which is where I got my start. Upon randomly discovering the cookies could float in liquid, I gave them the nickname "floaties"! I thought they looked so cute when floating, so I decided I wanted to give it a go and started making all kinds of fun-shaped designs and animals.

I posted the first meringue cookie videos on my social media and they were not a hit right off the bat, but after someone requested the recipe and directions on how to recreate them, things took off. My most popular designs now have millions of views—people seemed to love them, and I started getting so many requests for new characters! I began with relatively easy designs, but now I create intricate characters, such as Shin Chan, Kung Fu Panda, Minions and dragons. I eventually branched out from there and started experimenting with other confections, such as my beloved character marshmallows and macarons.

Since then, I have received so many questions from my followers about the recipe or problems they encounter when making them—and now I am finally able to compile all my best tips and tricks into a book! This is an in-depth beginner's guide for making character meringue cookies, macarons and marshmallows. With over 50 adorable designs, it includes a variety of recipes for every degree of skill, ranging from beginner to advanced level, so you can experiment with more intricate designs once you've mastered the techniques.

The special troubleshooting sections will give you all the tips and tricks needed to create your favorite character treats and the step-by-step illustrations will make it easier to follow the instructions. The book also includes templates for all the macaron designs used in these projects. Perhaps best of all, there are designs for any occasion!

Even though the ingredients might seem simple, the craftsmanship behind meringue cookies, macarons and marshmallows is what makes them unique. These designs will cover all the basics you need to know to be able to make any character you want in the future. I guarantee that once you get the hang of it, you will be hooked! Now, let's get started.

ESSENTIAL KITCHEN EQUIPMENT AND INGREDIENTS

To achieve the best possible results, it is key to understand the equipment and ingredients you are working with, since baking depends on many variables, which can all create different outcomes.

STAND MIXER OR HAND MIXER: The recipes in this book require a fair amount of mixing. I prefer using a hand mixer when working with small quantities, to make sure you get to the bottom of the bowl, which you often can't reach by using a stand mixer. However, when working with larger quantities, I'd suggest using a stand mixer, if you have one. I specify which type of mixer to use at different points throughout each recipe.

FOOD SCALE: Because of how precise the ingredient amounts need to be to create meringues, macarons and marshmallows, I recommend using a digital food scale, set to metrics (grams), to measure out the precise weight of your ingredients. These are widely available online and at grocery or kitchenware stores, and there are relatively inexpensive options that will get the job done for the recipes in this book.

CANDY THERMOMETER: When making marshmallows or meringue, it is crucial for the temperatures to be precise. Being even slightly off can change or ruin the entire outcome, so check your temperatures by using a candy thermometer. They are widely available in stores and online, and are relatively inexpensive.

SPATULA: Spatulas are used frequently in my recipes, and it's important to be aware that there are different types of spatulas. Some are resistant to high temperatures, but some are not. For making meringues and macarons, it doesn't matter which type of spatula you use. However, when making marshmallows, use a heat-resistant spatula, especially when making the sugar syrup!

PIPING TIPS: You'll use piping tips in all the meringue and macaron recipes in this book. All the piping tips mentioned are from the Wilton® brand, though you're welcome to use comparable tips from your preferred brand, if you like.

PIPING BAGS: You'll use piping bags in pretty much every recipe or design in this book. I use 12-inch (30-cm) piping bags, and it doesn't matter which brand of bag you use.

BAKING SCRIBERS: A baking scriber is a sharp, pointy tool, often used in cookie decorating to redistribute icing, smooth the tops of macaron batter or to redistribute meringue. It is a perfect tool for doing detailed work. You can find them in some baking shops or online stores, such as Amazon.

DOUGH SCRAPER: I use this tool, also known as a bench scraper or pastry scraper, for leveling out the cornstarch when making marshmallows.

PARCHMENT PAPER: I use this to line baking sheets and to pipe designs onto—especially when making meringue cookies, since I can easily cut it into smaller pieces. In my Basic Meringue Recipe for Character Meringue Cookies (page 10), I will further explain why.

TEFLON® SHEET: A Teflon sheet is similar to parchment paper, but thicker and reusable. I like to use this surface when making macarons since it also gives it a smooth finish.

SILICONE BAKING MAT: This is the thickest material of the three pan liners. The baking mat contains a layer of fiberglass mesh covered with silicone. I often also use this for making macarons.

GEL FOOD COLORING: Gel food coloring plays an important role in this book, as you'll need this to add color to your designs. Why gel? Because it will not affect the texture of your meringue as much as liquid food coloring does, and the colors are much more concentrated. Throughout this book, I use Wilton brand gel food coloring, but you can use any other brand. Just keep in mind the pigmentation of each brand may differ and may affect the outcome of the recipes.

SUPERFINE OR GRANULATED SUGAR: Not surprisingly, all the recipes in this book call for sugar—usually superfine. The crystals of superfine sugar are more finely ground than those of granulated sugar, which means it dissolves faster than granulated sugar. It's readily available in the United States; in the United Kingdom, this is known as caster sugar.

POWDERED SUGAR: Many recipes in this book also call for powdered sugar (also known as icing sugar or confectioners' sugar). Basically, it is granulated or superfine sugar that has been crushed into a fine powder.

EDIBLE MARKERS: Edible markers are a great tool for making small details if you are new to baking. They can be used for drawing on macarons, meringue cookies or marshmallows. You can find edible markers in many baking shops.

CORNSTARCH: Cornstarch is used throughout the marshmallow chapter; you'll cover your marshmallows in cornstarch so they don't stick. It can be found in pretty much any supermarket, but keep in mind that cornstarch and corn flour are two totally different ingredients! Be sure what you are using is cornstarch!

PAINTBRUSHES: Are you surprised to see paintbrushes listed here? They're used for covering marshmallows in cornstarch in the marshmallows chapter (page 127). Any small, clean paintbrush can be used for this; just make sure the bristles are soft.

CORN SYRUP: Light corn syrup is used for making marshmallows, as it helps to prevent crystals from forming in the cooled syrup. If it's difficult to find corn syrup, on page 131 you will find several alternatives that you could use instead.

GELATIN SHEETS: These are made from gelatin that is dried in a flat sheet. You'll need them to make the designs in the marshmallows chapter (page 127).

FUN MERINGUE
Friends and Floaties

You might have seen meringue cookies, which I also often refer to as floaties, all over my social media! The reason they are named floaties is that they can float in liquid, such as coffee or hot chocolate, which makes them jiggle so cutely in the cup.

If you have never had one, meringue cookies are light, airy treats with a crisp exterior. Basically, meringue is made from egg whites, sugar and a flavored extract whipped together. In this chapter, I share my classic vanilla meringue recipe, but you could use different flavored extracts to add your own twist. I've included several suggestions to choose from, if you'd like.

Once you whip up this Basic Meringue Recipe (page 10), you can go straight to the design of your choice and add the food colors according to the recipes. You can now recreate my lovely frogs (page 27), charming hanging cats (page 33) or maybe my most popular floaties, the adorable little dachshunds (page 23), yourself!

Once you're done making them, you can eat them right away or have them in your cup of coffee, milk or hot chocolate. They will not melt fully as marshmallows do, but you can dip them just like cookies into your drink and eat them separately.

BASIC MERINGUE RECIPE

FOR CHARACTER MERINGUE COOKIES

Yield: 16 to 18 pieces
1½ inches (4 cm) each

INGREDIENTS AND TOOLS

35 g fresh egg whites

60 g superfine sugar

½ tsp vanilla extract or other flavored extract

Scant 2 tbsp (15 g) powdered sugar (see Note)

Gel food coloring of choice

Stand mixer

Candy thermometer

Meringue is basically egg whites and sugar. However, you can add a few other ingredients, such as flavored extracts, lemon juice or even powdered freeze-dried fruit! To create meringue cookies, we need to make a stable meringue. You know your meringue is stable enough when, as you lift the whisk, the meringue forms a stiff and pointy peak with just a slight bend at the end. You'll also be able to hold the bowl upside down above your head without anything falling out.

Although the ingredients for meringue might seem simple, the technique of making it can be quite challenging. But with this recipe and the troubleshooting tips on page 12, you will be able to whip this up without a problem.

Meringue can be made in various ways. I personally prefer to use the Swiss method, which basically means heating egg whites and sugar together, using a double boiler, until the sugar dissolves. It makes a very stable meringue and gives it a nice glossy finish.

LET'S GET STARTED!

1. Begin by making sure all your tools are super clean. This is very important! The bowl of your stand mixer, whisk and spatula should not have any traces of grease, or your egg whites will not whip up properly. Wash your tools in hot, soapy water and dry them well, or use a small amount of vinegar to wipe down your equipment before using.

2. When separating your egg whites, make sure you do this very carefully so there are no traces of egg yolk in your egg whites. If this happens, unfortunately you will have to start over again with other eggs, as even a little bit of yolk will make it impossible to whip your egg whites to stiff peaks. Place the egg whites and superfine sugar in the bowl of a stand mixer.

3. In a saucepan, bring about 1 inch (2.5 cm) of water to a simmer over medium heat.

4. Once the water is simmering, place the bowl of egg whites and sugar on top of the saucepan; the bottom of the bowl should not touch the water! The steam will be enough to heat the egg whites and sugar.

5. Use a candy thermometer to keep an eye on the temperature and stir constantly with a spatula. When the egg whites have reached 115°F (45°C), remove your bowl immediately from the heat. Do not overheat your egg whites! I heat my egg whites until they are 120°F (50°C), but already remove them from the heat at 115°F (45°C). The remaining heat from the bowl will continue to heat the mixture.

6. Keep mixing with a spatula for 2 to 3 minutes to slowly bring down the temperature of the egg whites and sugar. The sugar should be completely dissolved and the mixture should look like a thick syrup.

7. After the mixture has cooled to about 75°F (24°C), transfer the bowl to your stand mixer. Using a whisk attachment, beat on medium-high speed for 8 to 10 minutes, or until the mixture has turned white and has slightly thickened, similar to the consistency of maple syrup.

8. Use a spatula to incorporate the vanilla and powdered sugar into the egg whites first, and then mix again on medium-high speed for 10 to 15 minutes, or until stiff peaks form (see Troubleshooting, page 12, for more on this). Your meringue should look smooth and glossy. When you take out the whisk, the meringue should be able to hold its shape with a slight bend at the top. The photo labeled 8A shows a meringue (with soft peaks) that is not yet stiff enough, while photo 8B shows a meringue (with stiff peaks) that is ready to use.

Your basic meringue is now done! Now, go to the project you will be using to follow the rest of the instructions.

NOTE: This recipe can simply be doubled, except for the powdered sugar. Add only 20 to 22 grams of powdered sugar (not another 60 grams) if you want to double the recipe.

5

6

8A

8B

TROUBLESHOOTING

In this section, I will discuss some of the issues that may occur when making meringue cookies and how to fix them. Keep in mind that your oven, ingredients, equipment and environment can influence the outcome of your meringue cookies.

WHAT SHOULD MY MERINGUE'S TEXTURE BE LIKE?

After making character meringues for a while, I have noticed different stages of meringue produce a different end result. For some designs, you want to use a softer meringue; for others, you need a very stiff meringue.

SOFT(ER) PEAKS: This is the stage where your meringue is soft but still holding its shape. I prefer using this type of meringue if I pipe flat characters (2-D) and if some details need to blend into the rest of the meringue. For example, if you are making spots on cows or the stripes on a zebra, you want to blend these colors together. If you use a very stiff meringue, it would be almost impossible to blend the colors seamlessly.

STIFF PEAKS: If you mix soft meringue for a few minutes longer on high speed, you will start to notice that it becomes a lot stiffer. If you take the whisk out and make little spikes, those little spikes should hold their shape. This stage and texture of meringue is great for piping small details that need to stand out, such as ears, horns or wings, and to create 3-D character meringues.

MY STIFF MERINGUE LOOKED GREAT, BUT NOW IT'S STARTED TO SOFTEN. WHAT HAPPENED?

Different factors could cause this problem.

- You have added too much food coloring (more than suggested) or used liquid food coloring instead of gel food coloring.

- You have beaten all the air out of your meringue when mixing in the gel food coloring. Try to beat your meringue carefully in a circular motion, starting from the bottom of the bowl and working your way up.

- Leaving your meringue out at room temperature for a long time as well as the heat from your hands will eventually soften the meringue. Try to work fast and don't hold the piping bags too long as in both cases, heat is the problem.

WHY ARE MY MERINGUE COOKIES BREAKING IN THE OVEN?

This is probably the most frequently asked question. It also depends on your oven, but one of the main reasons your meringues could break in the oven is that you have let them air-dry for too long. The ones that were made first have slowly started to dry on the outside and have formed a "shell." So, when you start to bake them, the inside of the meringues starts to expand slightly (because of the temperature difference), causing them to burst open and break. To prevent this, all of the recipes in this book call for you to make and bake the meringues immediately. For example, once you're done piping two lion meringues, place them in the oven immediately and continue making two more lion meringues. Once these two are done, place them in the oven with the other two made earlier, until all 12 lion meringues are in the oven, and then bake them for 60 more minutes.

Another reason might be that your oven temperature is set too high; it is important to bake the meringues at a low temperature. I prefer starting at a low temperature so they can slowly bake and harden on the outside, then increase the temperature to bake the insides further. This has worked best for me to minimize breakage.

WHAT IF MY OVEN TEMPERATURE CANNOT GO LOWER THAN 210°F (100°C)?

In this case, use a different method to make your meringue cookies. Instead of cutting your parchment paper into four 6-inch (15-cm) squares, cut them into smaller pieces to fit one meringue cookie per piece. Pipe one meringue character at a time and transfer them directly into the oven. This way, the temperature matters less—the meringue cookies don't air-dry on the outside, thus minimizing the risk of breakage.

HOW CAN I MAKE MY MERINGUE COOKIES FLOAT?

Most of the meringue cookies in this book are designed to float in a cup of your favorite beverage (with a few exceptions—the hanging cats [page 33] and monkeys [page 42] are great to hang on mugs and cups, while the elephants [page 51] and princesses [page 47] are fun to decorate cakes with!).

After making so many meringue cookies, I was always so excited when they were done and then got so disappointed when I wanted to make them float in a drink and just saw them sink. As a rule of thumb: Tall and narrow meringue cookies will not float or may lean and sink toward one side, but low and broad meringue cookies will float! So, if you want your meringue cookies to float in liquid, make sure the base of the cookies is broad and do not make them too tall.

HOW DO I STORE MY MERINGUE COOKIES?

It is important you store your meringues in an airtight container in a cool environment, especially when the weather is very rainy or humid. Have your meringue cookies become sticky while they were totally fine when coming out of the oven? That is because they have slowly reabsorbed moisture from the air. Therefore, it is important to store them well! When stored well, the meringue cookies have a shelf life of about three weeks.

LOVELY LIONS

Difficulty level: Intermediate
Yield: 12 cookies
about 1½ inches (4 cm) tall

These cute lions are great for a safari-themed birthday party. Use them as cake toppers or to decorate cupcakes, or you could pack them individually as little gifts to your guests.

The trickiest parts about this character are the head and mane of the lion, so make sure you work with a very stiff meringue. If your meringue is too soft, the mane will not hold its shape and eventually will either collapse or become one messy blob. For extra tips on different textures of meringue, see Troubleshooting (page 12).

Begin by making one batch of the Basic Meringue Recipe on page 10 and make sure you have the following colors ready:

INGREDIENTS AND TOOLS

Brown, orange, yellow and black gel food coloring

6 piping bags

1 #7 round piping tip

1 #6 round piping tip

1 #2A round piping tip

Baking sheet

6 (4-inch [10-cm]) squares parchment paper

Baking scriber or toothpicks

PREP THE COLORS

When mixing in the gel food coloring, try to keep the airy texture of the meringue as much as possible.

BROWN: Place one-quarter of the meringue in a mixing bowl and add 4 to 5 drops of brown gel food coloring and 2 drops of orange gel food coloring to give some warmth to the color. Mix, using a small spoon or spatula, and transfer to a piping bag fitted with round piping tip #7.

ORANGE: Place half of the remaining meringue in a separate mixing bowl and add 4 to 5 drops of orange gel food coloring and 2 drops of yellow gel food coloring. Mix, using a small spoon or spatula, and transfer one-quarter of the orange meringue to a piping bag fitted with round piping tip #6. Transfer the other three-quarters of the orange meringue to a piping bag fitted with round piping tip #2A.

Now, divide the remaining meringue equally among three separate mixing bowls to make the following colors:

BLACK: To the first portion, add 4 to 6 drops of black gel food coloring. Mix in the color, using a small spoon or spatula, and transfer to a separate piping bag (no piping tip required).

LIGHT BROWN: To the second portion, add 1 drop of brown gel food coloring. Mix in the color, using a small spoon or spatula. Transfer to a piping bag (no piping tip required).

WHITE: The third portion of meringue can be transferred directly to a piping bag with no piping tip. (No food coloring required.)

(continued)

LOVELY LIONS
(CONTINUED)

PIPE THE LIONS

1. Preheat your oven to 160°F (70°C) and place a baking sheet on the middle rack.

2. We will be making two lions at a time per parchment square. Using the orange meringue fitted with round piping tip #2A, pipe two semicircles onto the parchment to create the body of a lion and a ball shape on top of it to create its head.

3. Now, using the brown meringue, pipe in small strokes to create the mane of each lion.

4. Cut a scant ¼-inch (6-mm) opening at the tip of the piping bag of light brown meringue. Use it to pipe on one snout per lion. Smooth out the edges, using a baking scriber or toothpick.

5. Next, take your orange meringue fitted with round piping tip #6 and pipe the front paws and ears per lion. Pipe the ears onto each lion's mane.

6. Make a tiny cut at the tip of the piping bag of black meringue and use it to pipe the eyes and a small dot on top of the snout per lion.

7. Dip your baking scriber into the black meringue of the eyes and add dots onto the snout and stripes on the ears.

8. Finish by adding two small dots onto the eyes, using white meringue. I prefer piping a little amount of white meringue onto my baking scriber and gently pressing it on to create these small dots.

9. After you have made two lions on a parchment square, transfer them directly into the oven to bake. Repeat the above steps, piping two lions at a time, until all 12 lions are in the oven.

BAKE THE FLOATIES

10. Once they are all in the oven, bake for 80 minutes. After 80 minutes, increase the oven temperature to 175°F (80°C) and bake for 40 minutes.

11. After baking them for 120 minutes (2 hours) in total, turn off the oven and let them sit in the oven for 20 minutes to continue the drying process.

FUN FLUFFY SHEEP

Difficulty level: Intermediate
Yield: 12 cookies
about 1½ inches (4 cm) each

INGREDIENTS AND TOOLS

Black gel food coloring

4 piping bags

1 #6 round piping tip

1 #10 round piping tip

1 #7 round piping tip

1 #2A round piping tip

Baking sheet

6 (4-inch [10-cm]) squares parchment paper

Baking scriber or toothpicks

Sheep come in many different colors, but for this design, we are going to make cute little white sheep with black faces. However, you can switch up the colors as you like!

In this project, you will need to use only one color of gel food coloring, but the execution can be tricky as the sheep has a lot of texture, especially the wool. Also important to keep in mind is that black-colored meringue bakes differently than white or light-colored meringue. Black meringue dries slower and thus needs longer to bake, so pay attention to the baking time and temperatures for this design!

Begin by making one batch of the Basic Meringue Recipe on page 10 and make sure you have the following colors ready:

PREP THE COLORS

When mixing in the gel food coloring, try to keep the airy texture of the meringue as much as possible.

BLACK: Place one-third of the meringue in a mixing bowl and add about 3 pea-sized drops of black gel food coloring. Carefully mix in the color, using a spatula. The color does not have to be pitch black; dark gray is sufficient. It is difficult to achieve black meringue, and if you add a lot of food coloring, it will only add more moisture, thus preventing your meringue from drying properly.

Transfer one-quarter of the black meringue to a piping bag fitted with round piping tip #6, and the remaining three-quarters of the black meringue to a piping bag fitted with round piping tip #10.

WHITE: Divide the remaining meringue between two piping bags, one-half to a piping bag fitted with round piping tip #7 and the other half to a piping bag fitted with round piping tip #2A. (No food coloring needed.)

(continued)

FUN FLUFFY SHEEP (CONTINUED)

PIPE THE SHEEP

1. Preheat your oven to 160°F (70°C) and place a baking sheet on the middle rack.

2. We will be making two sheep per parchment square. Using the white meringue fitted with round piping tip #2A, pipe a ball shape about ¾ inch (2 cm) high and wide to make each sheep's body.

3. Now, take the black meringue fitted with round piping tip #10 and pipe the face of a sheep onto each white ball of meringue. Smooth out the edges, using a baking scriber or toothpick.

4. Next, take the white meringue fitted with piping tip #7 and pipe small round shapes all around the body of each sheep, to create the texture of the wool.

5. Use the same white meringue to pipe two small white dots on each face to create the eyes.

6. Then, use the black meringue fitted with round piping tip #6 to pipe the ears and little feet (front and back) of each sheep.

7. Finally, use the same black meringue fitted with round piping tip #6 to pipe on the eyes. Dip your baking scriber into white meringue to add small white dots onto the eyes to create that cute glossy look.

8. After you have made two sheep on a parchment square, transfer them carefully into the oven. Repeat the above steps, piping two sheep at a time, until all 12 sheep are in the oven.

BAKE THE FLOATIES

9. Once all 12 sheep are in the oven, bake them for 80 minutes. After 80 minutes, increase the oven temperature to 185°F (85°C) and bake for 45 minutes.

10. After baking them for 125 minutes in total, turn off the oven and let them sit in the oven for 25 minutes to continue the drying process. Take them out of the oven and allow them to cool completely.

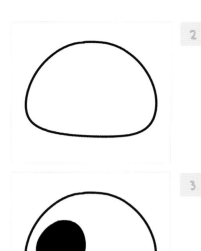

SAFARI ZEBRAS

Difficulty level: Intermediate
Yield: 16 cookies
about 1½ inches (4 cm) each

INGREDIENTS AND TOOLS

Black gel food coloring

Gray gel food coloring (optional)

4 piping bags

2 #7 round piping tips

1 #5 round piping tip

1 #2A round piping tip

Baking sheet

4 (6-inch [15-cm]) squares parchment paper

Baking scriber or toothpicks

Zebras were my favorite safari animal when I was a kid, so I had to include them in the book. We are going to make them in 2-D as opposed to 3-D because I want to focus on the entire body of the zebra. Making 3-D characters is possible, but I would suggest doing it only if the shape of the design is round or if you only want to create the head. For this zebra, I found the 2-D design cuter and a lot more visible when dropping them into a drink.

Make sure your meringue is not whipped too stiff for this design (see page 12 for more information on this) as it includes a lot of details that need to blend together, such as the stripes and muzzle of the zebra.

Before we get started, begin by making one batch of the Basic Meringue Recipe on page 10 and make sure you have the following colors ready:

PREP THE COLORS

When mixing in the gel food coloring, try to keep the airy texture of the meringue as much as possible.

GRAY: Take 1 tablespoon (15 ml) of meringue and add 2 drops of black gel food coloring or 3 to 4 drops of gray gel food coloring. Often gray gel food coloring has a cooler, earthier tone than black gel food coloring, but either will work. Mix in the color, using a small spoon or spatula, and transfer to a piping bag fitted with one round piping tip #7.

BLACK: Place one-fifth of the remaining meringue in a mixing bowl and add 2 pea-sized drops of black gel food coloring. Mix in the color, using a small spoon or spatula. Depending on how pigmented your black food coloring is, add 2 to 3 drops more to intensify the color, if needed. The meringue does not have to be pitch black; dark gray is good enough! Transfer it to a piping bag fitted with round piping tip #5.

WHITE: Divide the remaining meringue between two piping bags: one-third to a piping bag fitted with the other round piping tip #7, and the remaining two-thirds to a piping bag fitted with piping tip #2A. (No food coloring required.)

(continued)

SAFARI ZEBRAS (CONTINUED)

PIPE THE ZEBRAS

1. Preheat your oven to 160°F (70°C) and place a baking sheet on the middle rack.

2. We will be making four zebras per parchment square. Onto one of the four parchment squares, using the white meringue with round piping tip #2A, pipe four oval shapes about 1¼ inches (3 cm) wide to create the body of each of the four zebras.

3. Then, with the same piping bag of white meringue, pipe a head, about ¾ inch (2 cm) long, onto the left top area of the body of each zebra. Smooth out the edges, using a baking scriber or toothpick.

4. Next, using the black meringue fitted with round piping tip #5, pipe on the mane of each zebra. Use a baking scriber to create sharp edges, and make sure not to make this part too thin, or else it will break easily when trying to peel the zebra off the parchment after baking.

5. Using black meringue again, pipe stripes over each body and on the upper half of each head.

6. Now, use your gray meringue to pipe the muzzle of each zebra. Blend this part into the white meringue, using your baking scriber.

7. Then, use the white meringue fitted with round piping tip #7 to pipe on the legs, ear and tail of each zebra. Use your baking scriber to adjust the shape, if needed.

8. Use black meringue to pipe on the hoofs and tail of each zebra, and finish off by dipping your baking scriber into black meringue to draw on the eye and nostrils.

9. After you have made four zebras on a parchment square, transfer them carefully to the oven and repeat the above steps again until all 16 zebras are in the oven.

BAKE THE FLOATIES

10. Bake your zebras for 60 minutes, then increase the oven temperature to 175°F (80°C) and bake for 60 minutes more.

11. After baking them for 120 minutes in total, turn off the oven and let them sit in the oven for 20 minutes to continue the drying process. Take them out of the oven and allow to cool completely.

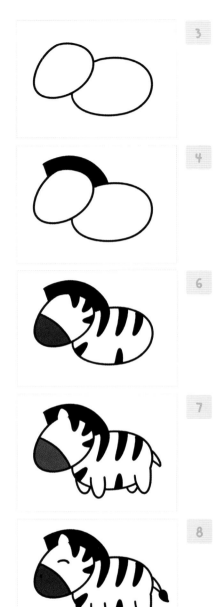

ADORABLE DACHSHUNDS

Difficulty level: Intermediate
Yield: 16 cookies
about 1½ inches (4 cm) each

INGREDIENTS AND TOOLS

Black gel food coloring (optional)

Brown gel food coloring

3 or 4 piping bags

2 #6 round piping tips

1 #12 round piping tip

Baking sheet

4 (6-inch [15-cm]) squares parchment paper

Baking scriber or toothpicks

Black edible marker (optional)

These adorable dachshunds are probably my most popular floaties ever, and you can now create these pups yourself!

The design itself is not that difficult; however, pay attention to the texture of your meringue. It should not be too soft (see page 12 for tips), or else the nose and paws will not hold their shape and would just blend away into the rest of the body. So, mix your meringue for a little longer if you are not sure if it's stiff enough, and do not use more food coloring than suggested in the directions. For a more beginner-friendly process, use a black edible marker, instead of black meringue, to make the details on the pups after they are baked and totally cooled.

Before we get started, begin by making one batch of the Basic Meringue Recipe on page 10 and have the following colors ready:

PREP THE COLORS

When mixing in the gel food coloring, try to keep the airy texture of the meringue as much as possible.

BLACK (SKIP THIS STEP IF USING AN EDIBLE BLACK MARKER): Take 1 tablespoon (15 ml) of meringue and add 5 to 7 drops of black gel food coloring. Gently mix in the color, using a small spoon or small spatula, then transfer to a piping bag. No piping tip is required.

BROWN: Place two-thirds of the remaining meringue in a mixing bowl and add 6 to 7 drops of brown gel food coloring. Carefully mix in the coloring, using a spatula, making sure you scrape all the sides and bottom well and using a circular motion working from top to bottom.

Also keep in mind that when baking the floaties, the colors will darken slightly. So, make them less brown than you actually want them to be.

After mixing in the color, transfer one-third of the brown meringue

to a piping bag fitted with one round piping tip #6, and the other two-thirds of the brown meringue to another piping bag fitted with round piping tip #12.

LIGHT BROWN: To the remaining meringue, add 4 to 5 drops of brown gel food coloring and gently mix, using a small spoon or spatula. The color should be slightly lighter than the brown you made earlier. When the color is fully incorporated, transfer to a piping bag fitted with the other round piping tip #6.

(continued)

ADORABLE DACHSHUNDS
(CONTINUED)

PIPE THE DACHSHUNDS

1. Preheat your oven to 160°F (70°C) and place a baking sheet on the middle rack.

2. We will make four dachshunds per parchment square. Onto one square, using the brown meringue fitted with round piping tip #12, pipe four sausage shapes about 1½ inches (4 cm) long, each with a slight bend in it, leaving 2 inches (5 cm) of space between them.

3. With the same piping bag, pipe a cone shape on the top part of the sausage shape to create the face of each dachshund. With your light brown meringue fitted with round piping tip #6, pipe the ears onto the sides of each head. Be cautious not to make the ears too thin, or else they will break easily. They should be at least a scant ¼ inch (6 mm) thick each.

4. Then, use the brown meringue fitted with round piping tip #6 to pipe four paws and a tail onto each dachshund. Make sure the bottom paws are large enough to add paw pads in a later step.

Go straight to step 6 if you want to use an edible marker to draw on the final details.

5. Lastly, make a small cut at the tip of your piping bag of black meringue. Pipe on the paw pads and dip a baking scriber or toothpick into black meringue to draw the facial features (eyes, nose and smile) onto each dachshund's head. This way, you will get much thinner lines as opposed to piping them on.

6. After you have made four dachshunds on a parchment square, gently transfer them directly into the oven to bake. Repeat the above steps until all 16 dachshunds are in the oven.

BAKE THE FLOATIES

7. Bake the dachshunds for 70 minutes, then increase the oven temperature to 175°F (80°C) and bake for another 45 minutes.

8. After baking them for 115 minutes in total, turn off the oven and let them sit in the oven for another 20 minutes to continue the drying process. Take them out of the oven and allow to cool completely. If using black edible marker, add the paw pads and facial details after the dachshunds have cooled completely.

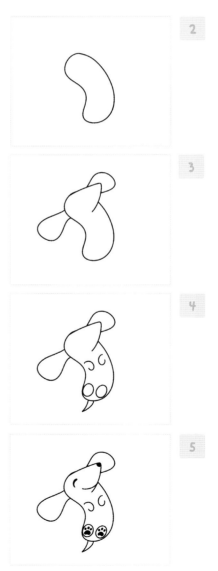

FROGS IN LOVE

Difficulty level: Beginner
Yield: 12 cookies
about 1½ inches (4 cm) each

INGREDIENTS AND TOOLS

Black, red and green gel food coloring

4 or 5 piping bags

2 #6 round piping tips

1 #2A round piping tip

Baking sheet

4 (6-inch [15-cm]) squares parchment paper

Baking scriber or toothpicks

Black edible marker (optional)

These cute frogs are one of the first meringue cookies I ever made, and they are very beginner-friendly—and very adorable!

The black details on the face and eyes can be made using black meringue, or if you are not too comfortable with that yet, using an edible marker. If you are going with an edible marker, make sure you let your meringues cool completely after baking and do not press the black ink too long onto the meringue—it will slowly soak up the liquid, which can create gaps in your meringue, and you definitely do not want that after working on them for hours! So, be cautious when using edible markers, and once you have the confidence, use meringue for the details instead!

Before we get started, begin by making one batch of the Basic Meringue Recipe on page 10 and make sure you have the following colors ready:

PREP THE COLORS

When mixing in the gel food coloring, try to keep the airy texture of the meringue as much as possible.

BLACK (SKIP THIS STEP IF USING EDIBLE MARKER): Take 1 tablespoon (15 ml) of meringue and add 4 to 6 drops of black gel food coloring. Depending on how pigmented your black food coloring is, add 2 to 3 drops more to intensify the color, if needed. The meringue does not have to be pitch black; dark gray is good enough! Transfer to a piping bag with no piping tip.

WHITE: Transfer 2 tablespoons (30 ml) of meringue directly to a piping bag fitted with one round piping tip #6. (No food coloring required.)

RED: To 1 tablespoon (15 ml) of the remaining meringue, add 4 to 5 drops of red gel food coloring and mix. Transfer to a piping bag with no piping tip.

GREEN: Finally, to the remaining meringue, add 5 to 7 drops of green gel food coloring. Carefully mix in the coloring, using a spatula, until fully incorporated.

Divide the green meringue into two different piping bags: one-third to a piping bag fitted with the other round piping tip #6, and the remaining two-thirds to another piping bag fitted with round piping tip #2A.

(continued)

FROGS IN LOVE (CONTINUED)

PIPE THE FROGS

1. Preheat your oven to 160°F (70°C) and place a baking sheet on the middle rack.

2. We'll be making three frogs on each parchment square. Onto one square, using the green meringue fitted with round piping tip #2A, pipe three ovals about 1¼ inches (3 cm) in height and diameter. Adjust the shape and edges, using a baking scriber or toothpick.

3. Now, use your white meringue fitted with round piping tip #6 to pipe two small pea-sized dots on top of the green meringue to create the eyes of each frog.

4. Then, make a small cut at the tip of the piping bag of red meringue to create a small opening. Pipe a heart onto the chest of each frog. Use a baking scriber or toothpick to adjust the shape a little.

5. Use the green meringue fitted with round piping tip #6 to pipe the legs and arms of all the frogs. Pipe the arms slightly over the sides of each heart so it looks as if the frog is holding it.

If you are more comfortable using an edible marker, skip step 6 and go to step 7.

6. Finally, take the piping bag of black meringue and cut the tip just enough for the mixture to be pipeable. Pipe two small dots onto the white meringue to color the center of each eye and then, using your baking scriber, dip into the black meringue and draw a smile on the frog. This way, you will create much finer lines as opposed to piping them.

7. After you have made three frogs on a parchment square, carefully transfer them into the oven to bake. Repeat the above steps until all 12 frogs are in the oven.

BAKE THE FLOATIES

8. Once all 12 frogs are in the oven, bake them for 60 minutes, then increase the oven temperature to 175°F (80°C) and bake for another 40 minutes.

9. After baking them for 100 minutes in total, turn off the oven and let them sit in the oven for another 20 minutes to continue the drying process. Take them out of the oven and allow to cool completely (or overnight). If using an edible marker, draw on the facial features of the frogs at this stage.

BEAUTIFUL SWANS IN A POND

Difficulty level: Intermediate
Yield: 12 cookies
about 1½ inches (4 cm) each

INGREDIENTS AND TOOLS

Orange gel food coloring

3 piping bags

1 #2 round piping tip

1 #6 round piping tip

1 #2A round piping tip

Baking sheet

5 (8-inch [20-cm]) squares parchment paper

Baking scriber or toothpicks

Black edible marker

Even if you are new to making meringue cookies, these swans are achievable to make, yet look very impressive and intricate! Even though the design might not be that difficult, the trickiest part of making these swans is balancing them. Creating swan-shaped meringues is one thing, but for them to be floatable in your drink is another. In this recipe, I will specifically explain how to make these beautiful swans float, but visit Troubleshooting on page 12 for more tips!

Want to make it look as if these swans are floating in a pond? Try using butterfly pea tea to create that beautiful natural blue color! You can find this product at most natural/organic supermarkets.

Before we get started, begin by making one batch of the Basic Meringue Recipe on page 10 and have the following colors ready:

PREP THE COLORS

When mixing in the gel food coloring, try to keep the airy texture of the meringue as much as possible.

ORANGE: Take 1 tablespoon (15 ml) of meringue and add 4 to 5 drops of orange gel food coloring. Mix in the color, using a small spoon or spatula, and transfer to a piping bag fitted with round piping tip #2.

WHITE: Transfer half of the remaining meringue to a piping bag fitted with round piping tip #6, and the other half of the meringue to a piping bag fitted with round piping tip #2A. (No food coloring required.)

PIPE THE SWANS

1. Preheat your oven to 175°F (80°C) and place a baking sheet on the middle rack.

(continued)

BEAUTIFUL SWANS IN A POND (CONTINUED)

2. Onto two of the five parchment squares, using the white meringue fitted with round piping tip #6, pipe 12 sets of wing feathers in total. Each set of feathers should include six overlapping feathers and should be about 1½ inches (4 cm) in diameter and a scant ¼ inch (6 mm) thick. Once they're all done, place them in the oven to bake for 40 minutes.

3. While the wing feathers bake, onto the third parchment square, using the same white meringue fitted with round piping tip #6, pipe 12 backward S-shaped figures with a ball shape at the top to create the neck and head of the swans.

4. Then, use the orange meringue fitted with round piping tip #2 to pipe a small beak onto each head. After these steps, transfer the swan heads into the oven with the feathers and bake for 25 minutes.

5. Once both the wings and the heads and necks are done baking (the wings for 40 minutes, and the heads and necks for 25 minutes), take the meringues, including the baking sheet, out of the oven and let them cool completely.

6. Place the remaining two parchment squares on the baking sheet and pipe 12 ovals about 1¼ inches (3 cm) in diameter to create the body of each swan, making sure to leave about 2 inches (5 cm) of space between them.

7. Time to assemble the swans! First, place the head of each swan in the middle of each oval and carefully press the wings onto the sides. Make sure the head of the swan is not leaning forward too much; otherwise, it will sink when put in liquid. Also, make sure the wings are standing up straight and do not lean toward one side. It is about creating balance and distributing the weight evenly if you want them to float!

BAKE THE FLOATIES

8. Once you have assembled all the swans, carefully place your baking sheet (with the swans) back in the oven on the middle rack. Bake them at 160°F (70°C) for 60 minutes, then increase the oven temperature to 175°F (80°C) and bake for another 25 minutes.

9. After baking the swans for 85 minutes in total, turn off the oven and let them sit in the oven for 30 minutes to continue the drying process. Take them out and cool completely before peeling them off the parchment.

10. Use an edible black marker to draw on the eyes of the swans, and they are done!

PURRR-FECT HANGING CATS

(TWO STYLES)

Difficulty level: Advanced
Yield: 12 cookies per design
about 1¼ inches (3 cm) each

INGREDIENTS AND TOOLS

Orange gel food coloring

Black or gray gel food coloring

6 piping bags

1 #3 round piping tip

2 #8 round piping tips

2 #2A round piping tips

Baking sheet

1 sheet parchment paper

3 (2-inch [5-cm]) square silicone cupcake molds

Baking scriber or toothpicks

If you are comfortable making meringue cookies, it is now time to create some meringue cats to hang from the rim of your cup! Here are two different designs: one for white-and-orange cats, and one for gray cats. Make a dozen of your preferred design, or mix and match the designs for some variety! For both, make sure to pay attention to the thickness and size of the mug you'll be using, as each cup or mug is different. Mine is 4 inches (10 cm) in diameter with a thin rim.

The most important part of making these hanging meringue cats, is to work with a very stiff meringue. If you are unsure, place a small dollop of meringue on a flat surface, such as a wooden spatula, piece of paper or plate, and tilt it to see whether it starts to shift and lean toward one side. If this is the case, mix your meringue longer and test it again. You know it is good to use when you can tilt the meringue without it moving.

Begin by making one batch of the Basic Meringue Recipe on page 10 and make sure you have the following colors ready:

PREP THE COLORS

When mixing in the gel food coloring, try to keep the airy texture of the meringue as much as possible.

ORANGE: Take 1 tablespoon (15 ml) of meringue and add 3 to 4 drops of orange gel food coloring. Mix in the color, using a small spoon or spatula, and transfer to a piping bag fitted with round piping tip #3.

DARK GRAY: Take 1 tablespoon (15 ml) of meringue and add 4 to 5 drops of black gel food coloring. Mix in the color, using a small spoon or spatula, and transfer to a piping bag with no piping tip.

(continued)

PURRR-FECT HANGING CATS (CONTINUED)

GRAY: Place one-half of the remaining meringue in a mixing bowl and add 5 to 6 drops of gray gel food coloring or 3 to 4 drops of black gel food coloring. Carefully mix in the color with a spatula. Transfer one-half of this gray meringue to a piping bag fitted with one round piping tip #8 and the other half to another piping bag fitted with one round piping tip #2A.

WHITE: Transfer one-half of the remaining meringue to a piping bag fitted with the other round piping tip #8, and the other half to a piping bag fitted with the other round piping tip #2A. (No food coloring required.)

PIPE THE CATS

WHITE-ORANGE CAT

1. Line a baking sheet with the parchment paper, cutting away any excess. Place the cupcake molds upside down on the baking sheet.

2. Make one white-and-orange cat at a time. Onto one side of a mold, use the white meringue fitted with round piping tip #2A to pipe a round ball about ½ inch (1.3 cm) in diameter for the body of the cat. Use a baking scriber or toothpick to smooth out any edges.

3. Use the white meringue fitted with round piping tip #8 to pipe the arms of the cat. This is a crucial step, as it is what makes the cat hang on to your cup! Make sure to pipe a scant ¼ inch (6 mm) over the edge so it has enough surface to hold on; also, do not make the arms too thin. They should be at least a scant ¼ inch (6 mm) thick, or else they will break when you peel them from the mold after baking.

4. Go back to the white meringue fitted with round piping tip #2A and pipe another round ball about ¾ inch (2 cm) in diameter on top of the body, to create the cat's head.

5. Next, use the orange meringue fitted with round piping tip #3 to pipe a semicircle on one side of the head and fill in this part to create a spot. Smooth out the spot, using a baking scriber, and pipe an ear onto that same side.

6. Go back to the white meringue fitted with round piping tip #8 and pipe the other ear onto the other side of the head. Then, pipe the back legs and tail of the cat. While piping the tail, push the end of it slightly upward with your baking scriber.

7. Our white cat is done! Repeat, making four cats on each silicone mold, for a total of 12 cats (or your preferred number, keeping in mind that each meringue batch makes 12 cookies).

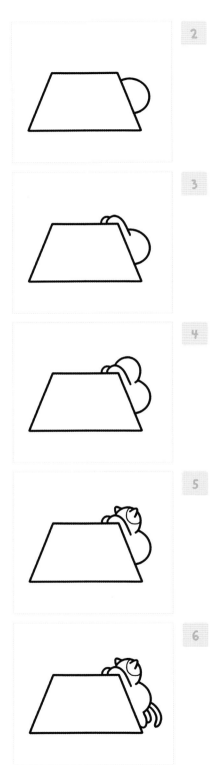

GRAY CAT

8. Line a baking sheet with parchment paper, cutting away any excess. Place the cupcake molds upside down on your baking sheet.

9. Make one gray cat at a time. Onto one side of a mold, use the gray meringue fitted with round tip #2A to pipe a round ball about ½ inch (1.3 cm) in diameter for the body of the cat. Use a baking scriber or toothpick to smooth out any edges.

10. Use the gray meringue fitted with round piping tip #8 to pipe the arms and legs of the cat. This is a crucial step, as this is what makes the cat hang on to your cup! Make sure to pipe a scant ¼ inch (6 mm) over the edge so it has enough surface to hold on; also, do not make the arms too thin. They should be at least a scant ¼ inch (6 mm) thick, or else they will break when you peel them from the mold after baking.

11. Go back to the gray meringue fitted with round piping tip #2A to pipe another round ball about ¾ inch (2 cm) in diameter, to create the cat's head.

12. Next, take the piping bag of dark gray meringue and make a small cut at the tip. Pipe a little of the dark gray meringue onto a baking scriber or toothpick and draw horizontal stripes onto the back of the cat and vertical lines on top of its head.

13. Use the gray meringue fitted with round piping tip #8 to pipe the ears and tail of the cat.

14. Our gray cat is done! Repeat, making four cats on each mold for a total of 12.

BAKE THE FLOATIES

15. After you have made all the cats, transfer your baking sheet with its molds to the middle rack of your oven. Turn your oven to 160°F (70°C) so the temperature slowly rises while they are baking, and bake for 80 minutes. After 80 minutes, increase the oven temperature to 185°F (85°C) and bake for 50 minutes.

16. After baking the cats for 130 minutes in total, turn off the oven and let them sit in the oven for 25 minutes to continue drying. Take them out and allow to cool for a few hours or overnight before peeling them off the molds.

HOW TO PEEL THEM OFF

17. Make sure they are fully dried, then start by gently peeling the body of a cat from the silicone mold (1). Next, carefully push the cat upward to detach the paws from the molds (2). Be careful not to break the paws, as this is what makes them hold on to your mug or cup. Repeat to remove the other cats from their molds. Now, you can hang your cats from your mug or cup!

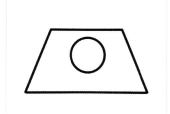

EMOJI FACES

Difficulty level: Beginner
Yield: 16 to 18 cookies
1¼ inches (3 cm) each

INGREDIENTS AND TOOLS

Yellow, red, blue and black gel food coloring

5 piping bags

1 #2A round piping tip

3 #2 round piping tips

4 (6-inch [15-cm]) squares parchment paper

Baking sheet

Baking scriber or toothpicks

Nowadays, we use emojis in our everyday life to express our feelings to others. Sometimes, you do not even have to use words; sending an emoji is enough to describe an emotion or expression. So, make these emoji faces and send them to your loved ones or surprise them with a fun emoji in their drink. You can be as creative as you would like, but in this book, we are going to cover three iconic emoji faces! The Cool emoji with shades, the Heart Eyes emoji and the LOL emoji.

Before we get started, begin by making one batch of the Basic Meringue Recipe on page 10 and make sure you have the following colors ready:

PREP THE COLORS

When mixing in the gel food coloring, try to keep the airy texture of the meringue as much as possible.

YELLOW: Place two-thirds of the meringue mixture in a mixing bowl and add 5 to 7 drops of yellow gel food coloring for a bright yellow shade. Carefully mix in the coloring, using a spatula, until fully incorporated. Transfer the mixture to a piping bag fitted with round piping tip #2A.

Now, divide the remaining meringue equally into four portions to create the following colors:

WHITE: Transfer one portion directly to a piping bag. (No piping tip or food coloring required.)

RED: Place the second portion in a mixing bowl. Add 3 to 4 drops of red gel food coloring and mix, using a small spoon or spatula, until fully incorporated. Once combined, it should be a bright red/pink color. Transfer to a piping bag fitted with one round piping tip #2.

BLUE: Place the third portion in a separate mixing bowl and add 3 to 4 drops of blue gel food coloring. Mix, using a small spoon or spatula, until fully incorporated, to create a bright blue color. Then, transfer to a piping bag fitted with another round piping tip #2.

BLACK: To the last portion of the meringue, add 5 to 6 drops of black gel food coloring. Carefully mix, using a small spoon or spatula. Depending on how pigmented your black food coloring is, add 2 to 3 drops more to intensify the color, if needed. The meringue does not have to be pitch black; dark gray is good enough! Transfer to a piping bag fitted with the remaining round piping tip #2.

(continued)

EMOJI FACES
(CONTINUED)

PIPE THE FACES

1. Preheat your oven to 160°F (70°C) and place a baking sheet on the middle rack.

2. Onto one parchment square, pipe four round disks about 1¼ inches (3 cm) in diameter and ½ inch (1.3 cm) thick, using the yellow meringue fitted with round piping tip #2A.

3. Pipe faces onto your meringue disks on the parchment paper:

For the Cool emoji, use the black meringue to pipe two dots where you want the sunglasses to be and use a baking scriber or toothpick to shape it into sunglasses. Finally, right below the sunglasses, pipe on a smile.

For the Heart Eyes emoji, use the red meringue to pipe two small hearts onto the face to create the eyes. Use a baking scriber or toothpick to adjust the shape a little, if needed. Use black meringue to pipe on the smile.

For the LOL emoji, use the black meringue to pipe a half-moon near an edge of a meringue disk to create the mouth. Take your piping bag of white meringue, make a small cut at the tip and pipe a white line on top of the black meringue to create the teeth. Then, use the black meringue to pipe on the eyes and dip your baking scriber into the black meringue to draw on thin lines for the eyebrows. Finally, using your blue meringue, pipe the tears.

4. After making four emoji faces on each parchment square, carefully place them on the baking sheet in the oven. Repeat until all your emoji faces are in the oven.

BAKE THE FLOATIES

5. When all your emoji faces are in the oven, bake them for 60 minutes. After 60 minutes, increase the oven temperature to 175°F (80°C) and bake for another 30 minutes.

6. After baking them for 90 minutes in total, turn off the oven and let them sit in the oven for another 20 minutes to continue the drying process. Take them out of the oven and allow to cool completely.

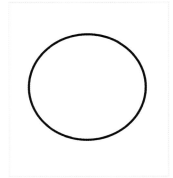

2

3A

3B

3C

COLORFUL LOLLIPOPS

Difficulty level: Beginner

Yield: 6 cookies
around 4 inches (10 cm) each

These colorful lollipops are an easy and fun treat you can make with kids. They do not require a lot of technique and you can personalize them by decorating them however you like, using edible glitter or sprinkles. For this design, we are going to use blue, purple, yellow and green, but you could make them in any color(s) of your choice. Wrap them individually to create a cute gift to hand out at birthday parties or other special events.

Before we get started, begin by making one batch of the Basic Meringue Recipe on page 10 and have the following colors ready:

Basic Meringue Recipe on page 10

INGREDIENTS AND TOOLS

Yellow, purple, blue and green gel food coloring

Plastic wrap

1 piping bag

1 #2D drop flower tip

Baking sheet

1 sheet parchment paper

6 cake pop sticks

Edible sprinkles and/or glitter, for decorating

Foil and ribbon (optional), for wrapping

PREP THE COLORS

When mixing in the gel food coloring, try to keep the airy texture of the meringue as much as possible. Divide the meringue equally among four mixing bowls to make the following colors:

YELLOW: To the first portion, add 4 to 5 drops of yellow gel food coloring. Mix in the coloring, using a small spoon or spatula, and set aside.

PURPLE: To the second portion, add 3 to 4 drops of purple gel food coloring. Mix in the coloring, using a small spoon or spatula, and set aside.

BLUE: To the third portion, add 3 to 4 drops of blue gel food coloring. Mix in the coloring, using a small spoon or spatula, and set aside.

GREEN: To the fourth portion, add 3 to 4 drops of green gel food coloring. Mix in the coloring, using a small spoon or spatula, and set aside.

(continued)

COLORFUL LOLLIPOPS (CONTINUED)

Now, we are going to assemble the colors. Spread out a 12-inch (30-cm) sheet of plastic wrap on your kitchen counter. Start at the bottom edge of the sheet with a horizontal line of the blue meringue. Then, on top of the blue, add a layer of the purple meringue, followed by one of the yellow meringue, then finish with a layer of the green meringue. Take both the top and bottom ends of the plastic wrap and gently roll the plastic into a sausage, pressing the four colors into a swirl. Transfer the roll of meringue (with its plastic wrap) to a piping bag fitted with drop flower tip #2D and it is ready to use!

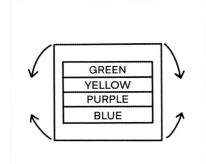

MAKE AND BAKE THE LOLLIPOPS

1. Preheat your oven to 160°F (70°C). Line a baking sheet with parchment paper, cutting away any excess.

2. Have your cake pop sticks ready. Working on one lollipop at a time, pipe a small dot of meringue onto the parchment and press the end of a cake pop stick onto it so it stays in place.

3. Pipe a swirl, starting from the center and working your way outward. The lollipop should be about 4 inches (10 cm) in diameter. You could leave it as is or add some sprinkles or edible glitter on top to jazz it up!

4. Repeat steps 2 and 3 to make the remaining lollipops. When you have made a full baking sheet of colorful lollipops, transfer the pan to the middle rack of the oven and bake for 60 minutes. After 60 minutes, increase the oven temperature to 185°F (85°C) and bake for another 60 minutes.

5. After baking the lollipops for 120 minutes in total, turn off the oven and let them sit in the oven for 25 minutes to continue the drying process.

After that, they are done! Make sure your lollipops are cooled completely before peeling them from the parchment paper. If you want to give them away as a gift, wrap them in foil and tie a ribbon into a bow around the bottom of the foil.

MONKEYS GOING BANANAS

(TWO STYLES)

Difficulty level: Advanced
Yield: 12 to 14 cookies
about 1¼ inches (3 cm) each

INGREDIENTS AND TOOLS

Black, light beige, yellow and brown gel food coloring

Pink gel food coloring (optional)

5 piping bags

2 #6 round piping tips

1 #4 round piping tip

1 #12 round piping tip

4 (6-inch [15-cm]) squares parchment paper

Baking sheet

2 (2-inch [5-cm]) square silicone cupcake molds

Baking scriber or toothpicks

For these cute monkeys, we are going to make two different designs: one, a hanging monkey; the other, to float in your drink. The hanging monkeys are slightly more difficult to make than the floating ones. So, if you are still getting comfortable with making meringue cookies, I would suggest you start with the floating monkeys first. You could also replace the black meringue for the details with a black edible marker, to make it more beginner-friendly.

Just as for the hanging cats (page 33), make sure your meringue is stiff enough to work with. How to test the texture of your meringue is explained on page 12.

Begin by making one batch of the Basic Meringue Recipe on page 10 and make sure you have the following colors ready:

PREP THE COLORS

When mixing in the gel food coloring, try to keep the airy texture of the meringue as much as possible.

BLACK: Take 1 teaspoon of meringue and add 4 to 5 drops of black gel food coloring. Mix in the color, using a small spoon or spatula, and transfer to a piping bag (no piping tip required).

LIGHT BEIGE: Take 1 tablespoon (15 ml) of meringue and add 3 to 4 drops of light beige gel food coloring. Alternatively, add 1 drop of brown gel food coloring and just the tip of a toothpick of pink gel food coloring. Mix in the color, using a small spoon or spatula, and transfer to a piping bag fitted with one round piping tip #6.

(continued)

MONKEYS GOING BANANAS (CONTINUED)

YELLOW: Take 1 tablespoon (15 ml) of meringue and add 3 drops of yellow gel food coloring. Mix in the color, using a small spoon or spatula, and transfer to a piping bag fitted with round piping tip #4.

BROWN: To the remaining meringue, add 5 to 6 drops of brown gel food coloring. Carefully mix in the color, using a small spoon or spatula. Transfer half of the brown meringue to a piping bag fitted with the other round piping tip #6, and the other half of the meringue to another piping bag fitted with round piping tip #12.

PIPE THE MONKEYS

If you start with the hanging monkeys, you do not have to preheat the oven. If you start with the floating monkeys, preheat the oven to 160°F (70°C) and skip to step 10.

1. First, we will make the hanging monkeys. Place two parchment squares side by side on the baking sheet and place a square silicone mold on top of each. Make sure the silicone molds are upside down with the bottom part facing up.

2. Make one monkey at a time. Using the brown meringue fitted with round piping tip #12, pipe onto one side of a silicone mold a round half circle about ¾ inch (2 cm) in diameter to create the body of the monkey.

3. Then, use the brown meringue fitted with round piping tip #6 to pipe on the arms and legs of the monkey. This is a very crucial step as it is what makes the monkey hang on to your cup! Make sure to pipe a scant ¼ inch (6 mm) over the edge so it has enough surface to hold on; also, do not make the arms too thin. They should be at least a scant ¼ inch (6 mm) thick, or else they will break easily when you try to peel them off the mold after baking.

4. Go back to the brown meringue fitted with piping tip #12 and pipe a ball shape on top of the body, to create the head of the monkey. It should be about ¾ inch (2 cm) in diameter.

5. Use the light beige meringue fitted with round piping tip #6 to pipe a heart shape in a thin layer onto the face. Use a baking scriber to smooth out the edges and to blend the color into the brown meringue. Then, use the same light beige meringue to pipe on the ears.

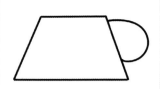

6. Use the yellow meringue fitted with round piping tip #4 to pipe a small banana peel on top of the head of the monkey.

7. Take your piping bag of black meringue and make a small cut at the tip. Dip your baking scriber into the black meringue to draw on the facial features of the monkey and add a small dot on the top part of the banana peel.

8. Lastly, use the brown meringue fitted with round piping tip #6 to pipe the tail of the monkey. Make two hanging monkeys on each silicone mold and transfer all four hanging monkeys, with their baking sheet, into the oven on the middle rack.

9. Turn your oven to 160°F (70°C) so the temperature slowly rises while they are baking. In the meantime, we are going to make our floating monkeys!

10. Take one of your remaining two pieces of parchment paper and use the yellow meringue fitted with piping tip #4 to pipe four bananas flat onto the parchment. The banana should be about 1 inch (2.5 cm) long, with about 2 inches (5 cm) of space between them. Adjust the shape a little, using your baking scriber.

11. Then, use your black meringue to add two small dots on each end of the banana and dip your baking scriber into the black meringue to draw a stripe on each banana.

12. Now, take your brown meringue fitted with round piping tip #12 and pipe a small ball right next to the banana to create the body of the monkey, then pipe a larger ball right above it to create the head. The head should slightly overlap the banana, but not the body. Repeat to create the other three floating monkeys.

13. Use the brown meringue fitted with round piping tip #6 to pipe on the arms and legs of each monkey, slightly over the banana, so it looks as if the monkey is hugging the banana.

14. Pipe a small amount of brown meringue onto your baking scriber and place this on top of the head to create little hairs of the monkeys.

15. Then, use light beige meringue fitted with round piping tip #6 to pipe the middle part of the face of each monkey, in a thin layer. Use your baking scriber to blend in the color and to smooth out the surface.

16. Dip your baking scriber into the black meringue and draw the facial features (eyes, nose and mouth) onto each monkey.

(continued)

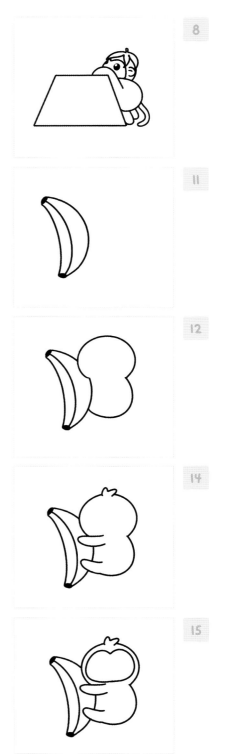

MONKEYS GOING BANANAS (CONTINUED)

17. Go back with light beige meringue to pipe on the ears and add two small dots onto the hands and feet of each monkey.

18. Lastly, go back to the brown meringue fitted with round piping tip #6 and pipe the tail of each monkey.

19. Repeat to make four floating monkeys on the remaining piece of parchment paper. Then carefully transfer them, on their parchment, to the baking sheet in the oven.

BAKE THE FLOATIES

20. The hanging monkeys should already have been in the oven for about 30 minutes, baking at 160°F (70°C). When the floating monkeys join them in the oven, bake all the monkeys together at 160°F (70°C) for 70 minutes.

21. After those 70 minutes are up, increase the oven temperature to 175°F (80°C) and bake for an additional 30 minutes.

22. When those 30 more minutes are up (the floating monkeys having baked for 100 minutes total; the hanging monkeys, placed in the oven earlier, for 130 minutes) turn off the oven and let them sit in the oven for 30 minutes to continue the drying process. Take them out of the oven and allow to cool completely.

HOW TO PEEL THEM OFF

23. Make sure they are fully dried! If you are unsure about it, let them air-dry for another day, especially if you live in a very hot and humid environment.

24. Start by carefully peeling back the body of the monkey. Then, carefully peel the arms of the monkey, pushing it upward. Repeat to remove the other monkeys.

17

18

24

FAIRY-TALE PRINCESSES

(A MULTIPLE PIECES DESIGN)

Difficulty level: Advanced
Yield: 8 cookies
about 2 inches (5 cm) each

INGREDIENTS AND TOOLS

Black, yellow, blue and light beige gel food coloring

7 piping bags

1 #2 round piping tip

3 #6 round piping tips

2 #2A round piping tips

4 (8-inch [20-cm]) squares parchment paper

Baking scriber or toothpicks

Baking sheet

Did you know you can stack and rebake your meringues? For the following two designs, we are going to make separate parts and assemble them afterward. Unlike the Beautiful Swans in a Pond (page 29) and Happy Thanksgiving Turkeys (page 65), we will create and build height to make the characters.

These princesses are so versatile and fun to make for special events, such as princess-themed birthday parties! You can design them however you like and work with any colors you like. They are also great to use to decorate cakes with or make individual princesses to top cupcakes.

As these princesses include a lot of detail and you need to bake them twice, they are more difficult to make. However, you can leave out some of the details and draw the final facial features using an edible black marker to make it more beginner-friendly.

Begin by making one batch of the Basic Meringue Recipe on page 10 and make sure you have the following colors ready:

PREP THE COLORS

When mixing in the gel food coloring, try to keep the airy texture of the meringue as much as possible.

BLACK: Take 1 teaspoon of meringue and add 4 to 5 drops of black gel food coloring. Mix in the color, using a spoon or spatula, and transfer to a piping bag (no piping tip required).

(continued)

FAIRY-TALE PRINCESSES (CONTINUED)

WHITE: Place 1 tablespoon (15 ml) of meringue directly into a piping bag fitted with round piping tip #2. (No food coloring required.)

YELLOW: Take 1 tablespoon (15 ml) of meringue and add 2 to 3 drops of yellow gel food coloring. Mix in the color, using a spoon or spatula, and transfer to a piping bag fitted with one round piping tip #6.

Divide the remaining meringue equally between two mixing bowls.

LIGHT BLUE: To one portion, add 2 to 3 drops of blue gel food coloring. Mix in the color, using a spoon or spatula, and transfer half of the blue meringue to a piping bag fitted with another round piping tip #6, and the other half in a different piping bag fitted with one round piping tip #2A.

LIGHT BEIGE: To the other portion, add 3 to 4 drops of light beige gel food coloring and carefully mix in, using a spoon or spatula. Transfer half of the light beige meringue to a piping bag fitted with the final round piping tip #6, and the other half to another piping bag fitted with the other round piping tip #2A.

PIPE THE PRINCESSES
MAKE THE BODY

1. Preheat your oven to 160°F (70°C). Use the light blue meringue fitted with round piping tip #2A to pipe four 1-inch (2.5-cm) ball shapes, each with a flat bottom, onto one parchment square. Repeat to pipe four more onto a second parchment square, making eight flat-bottomed balls in total. These form the princesses' dresses.

2. Next, use the light blue meringue fitted with round piping tip #6 to pipe the shoulders and draping on the dress (you can add your own twist to those!).

3. Now, use the white meringue fitted with round piping tip #2 to pipe small dots onto the shoulders, dress and neck area to create a pearl necklace. Smooth out any edges, using a baking scriber or toothpick.

4. Make sure to level out the top part of the body, so the head will stay put when you assemble the pieces together later.

5. Using the light beige meringue fitted with round piping tip #6, pipe on the hands of each princess. The body parts are now done! Carefully transfer the eight princess bodies, on the baking sheet, to the oven to bake on the middle rack for 50 minutes. After 50 minutes, take them out to cool.

(continued)

FAIRY-TALE PRINCESSES (CONTINUED)

MAKE THE HEAD

6. Use the light beige meringue fitted with round piping tip #2A to pipe four ball shapes (of similar size as the body) onto each of the other two parchment squares, leaving 1½ inches (4 cm) between the heads. Smooth out the edges, using a baking scriber or toothpick. You will have a total of eight heads.

7. Then, use the light beige meringue fitted with round piping tip #6 to pipe a small dot in the middle of each face to create the nose, and on the sides of each head for the ears.

8. Use the yellow meringue fitted with round piping tip #6 to pipe on the hair of each princess. I gave my princess an up-do!

9. Then, use the light blue meringue fitted with round piping tip #6 to create a headband on each princess.

10. Make a small cut at the tip of the piping bag of black meringue. Pipe two small dots onto the face to create the eyes. The nose should be right in the center between them.

11. Use your baking scriber to dip into the black meringue of the eyes and draw on the eyebrows, lashes and smile. This way, you will be able to create very thin lines.

12. The heads of the princesses are now done! Transfer them directly into the oven, onto the baking sheet, to bake on the middle rack for 50 minutes.

HOW TO ASSEMBLE

13. Once the body and head parts are both done baking, take them out of the oven (including the baking sheet) and let them cool.

14. Place the eight body parts on your baking sheet, keeping 2 inches (5 cm) of space between them. Pipe a pea-sized amount of light beige meringue on top of the body and stick the head on top of it.

15. Carefully transfer the baking sheet with the princesses into the oven on the middle rack and bake them at 160°F (70°C) for 50 minutes, then increase the oven temperature to 175°F (80°C) and bake for 30 more minutes.

16. After baking the princesses for 80 minutes in total, turn your oven off and let them sit in the oven for 30 more minutes to continue the drying process.

ADORABLE ELEPHANTS

(A MULTIPLE PIECES DESIGN)

Difficulty level: Advanced
Yield: 8 cookies
about 2 inches (5 cm) each

INGREDIENTS AND TOOLS

Black, gray and blue gel food coloring

4 piping bags

1 #7 round piping tip

1 #2A round piping tip

4 (8-inch [20-cm]) squares parchment paper

Baking scriber or toothpicks

Baking sheet

These cute elephants are another design that is twice baked for added height!

The trickiest part of creating the elephant is paying attention to the piping technique for the ears, and making sure you level out the surfaces where you stack the head onto the body, to keep them from falling apart when you move or bake them. But no worries; we will go through the steps together!

Begin by making one batch of the Basic Meringue Recipe on page 10 and make sure you have the following colors ready:

PREP THE COLORS

When mixing in the gel food coloring, try to keep the airy texture of the meringue as much as possible.

BLACK: Take 1 tablespoon (15 ml) of meringue and add 5 to 6 drops of black gel food coloring. Mix in the color, using a spoon or spatula, and transfer to a piping bag (no piping tip required).

WHITE: Place 1 tablespoon (15 ml) of meringue directly in a piping bag. (No piping tip or food coloring required.)

GRAY: To the remaining meringue, add 5 drops of gray gel food coloring plus 1 drop of blue food coloring. Alternatively, add 2 drops of black gel food coloring and 1 drop of blue gel food coloring.

Carefully mix in the color, using a spoon or spatula. Transfer one-half of the gray meringue to a piping bag fitted with round piping tip #7, and the other half to another piping bag fitted with round piping tip #2A.

(continued)

ADORABLE ELEPHANTS (CONTINUED)

PIPE THE ELEPHANTS

MAKE THE BODY

1. Preheat your oven to 160°F (70°C). Using the gray meringue fitted with round piping tip #2A, pipe four 1-inch (2.5-cm) ball shapes, each with a flat bottom, onto a square of parchment paper. Repeat on a second square of parchment paper, making eight flat-bottomed balls in total.

2. Now, use the gray meringue fitted with round piping tip #7 to pipe on the legs of each elephant. Smooth out any edges, using a baking scriber or toothpick.

3. Make a small cut at the tip of the piping bag of white meringue. Pipe a small amount of white meringue onto your baking scriber and press three small dots onto the ends of each foot to mimic the nails of each elephant.

4. Use your baking scriber to level out the top part of each elephant's body (where the head is going to be placed). Try to make the top part as straight as possible, as this is very crucial when assembling both parts at the end.

5. The body parts are now done! Now, carefully transfer them into the oven on a baking sheet on the middle rack to bake for 50 minutes. At the 50-minute point, take them out to cool.

MAKE THE HEAD

6. Use the gray meringue fitted with piping tip #2A to pipe four ball shapes (similar size as the body) onto a parchment square, leaving 2 inches (5 cm) of space between the balls, to create the head of the elephants. Repeat on a second parchment square, for a total of eight heads. Smooth out the edges, using a baking scriber or toothpick.

7. Use the gray meringue fitted with round piping tip #7 to pipe on the ears. To do this, start at the bottom and slowly, in a zigzag motion, go upward to create each ear. Then, use a baking scriber or toothpick to adjust the shape, if needed.

(continued)

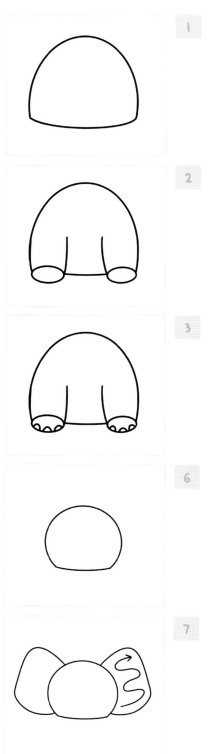

ADORABLE ELEPHANTS (CONTINUED)

8. Use the same gray meringue fitted with round piping tip #7 to pipe a trunk onto each elephant head. Pipe a small amount of gray meringue onto your baking scriber and draw horizontal lines on the trunk.

9. Using the same technique, pipe a small amount of gray meringue onto your baking scriber and make small hairs on top of each elephant's head.

10. Now, make a small cut at the tip of the piping bag with black meringue, just enough for the mixture to come out. Pipe on the eyes of the elephant, then dip your baking scriber into the black meringue to draw on the eyebrows.

11. Finally, pipe a small amount of white meringue onto your baking scriber and add two small dots onto the eyes to create that cute glossy look.

12. The head parts are now done! Transfer them carefully into the oven onto the baking sheet to bake for 50 minutes.

HOW TO ASSEMBLE

13. After the body and head parts have been in the oven for 50 minutes, take them out of the oven (including the baking sheet) and let them cool completely before peeling off the parchment. Place the two remaining parchment squares on the baking sheet. We are going to assemble two elephants on each square (four in total).

14. Pipe a small amount of gray meringue on top of a body part and carefully place a head part on top of it. Make sure they are well centered, so the head won't fall off. Repeat to assemble all eight elephants.

15. Carefully place the baking sheet on the middle rack of the oven. Bake again, for 30 minutes at 160°F (70°C), then increase the temperature to 175°F (80°C) and bake for 20 more minutes.

16. Once the elephants are finished baking, turn your oven off and let them sit in the oven for 30 minutes to continue the drying process.

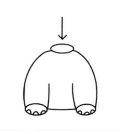

SPRING FLOWER BOUQUET

⇒ Difficulty level: Intermediate ⇐
⇒ Yield: 8 cookies ⇐
⇒ about 3 inches (7.5 cm) each ⇐

These beautiful edible flowers are a fun gift to give to your loved ones. You can basically make any type of flower and even combine them with different flowers or colors to make a bouquet, or wrap them individually.

For this design, you will need a specific piping tip to make the flower petals and leaves. If you do not have any of the flower petal or leaf piping tips needed for this design, just pipe the flower petals using a small round piping tip, then shape them into petals, using a baking scriber. It might not give you the exact same results, but your flowers will be just as beautiful!

Begin by making one batch of the Basic Meringue Recipe on page 10 and make sure you have the following colors ready:

INGREDIENTS AND TOOLS

Pink, yellow and green gel food coloring

3 piping bags

2 #103 petal piping tips

1 #70 leaf piping tip

Baking sheet

1 sheet parchment paper

Sprinkles (small round balls) of choice

8 cake pop sticks

PREP THE COLORS

Divide the meringue into three equal portions among three different mixing bowls. When mixing in the gel food coloring, try to keep the airy texture of the meringue as much as possible.

PINK: To the first portion, add 2 to 3 drops of pink gel food coloring and mix in the color, using a spatula. This should become light pink, rather than bright pink. Transfer to a piping bag fitted with one petal piping tip #103.

YELLOW: To the second portion, add 2 to 3 drops of yellow gel food coloring and use a spatula to mix in the color. Transfer to a piping bag fitted with the other petal piping tip #103.

GREEN: To the third portion, add 5 to 6 drops of green gel food coloring and mix in the coloring, using a spatula. Preferably, use a darker (forest) green opposed to bright green, to mimic the color of real leaves. Transfer the green meringue to a piping bag fitted with leaf piping tip #70.

(continued)

SPRING FLOWER BOUQUET
(CONTINUED)

PIPE THE FLOWERS

1. Line a baking sheet with the parchment paper, cutting away any excess. This way, we have an even surface to work with.

2. Make one flower at a time until you have eight in total. To do this, pipe a small dot of pink meringue onto the parchment paper. Press a cake pop stick on top of it so it stays in place. Pipe on flower petals, using an M-shaped piping technique. Go around until all of the petals are made—you should be able to fit about six petals per flower.

3. Then, use the yellow meringue to do the exact same thing on top of the pink flower petals, but making the yellow petals smaller and in the center of the pink flower. You should be able to fit about four yellow petals per flower.

4. Add sprinkles to the center of the flowers.

5. Lastly, add some green leaves, using the green meringue fitted with leaf piping tip #70. Keep repeating these steps until you have a full baking sheet of eight meringue flowers.

BAKE THE FLOWERS

6. Transfer the baking sheet with its flowers onto the middle rack of the oven and turn on the oven temperature to 160°F (70°C). *Do not preheat the oven; we want to bake them at a slow pace.* Bake for 70 minutes.

7. After baking the flowers for 70 minutes, increase the oven temperature to 175°F (80°C) and bake for 50 more minutes.

8. After baking them for 120 minutes in total, turn the oven off and let your meringue flowers sit in the oven for another 25 minutes.

9. When the flowers are fully cooled, gently peel them off the parchment paper and either wrap them as gifts or eat right away.

VALENTINE BEARS

~ Difficulty level: Beginner ~
~ Yield: 16 cookies ~
about 1¼ inches (3 cm) each ~

INGREDIENTS AND TOOLS

Black, red and brown gel food coloring

Yellow gel food coloring (optional)

4 piping bags

2 #6 round piping tips

1 #2A round piping tip

Baking sheet

4 (6-inch [15-cm]) squares parchment paper

Baking scriber or toothpicks

These meringue cookies are a great beginner-level design since they are piped flat. This way, you can see them well when they are floating on top of your hot chocolate, milk or coffee. You could make these for your loved ones on special occasions, such as Valentine's Day, their birthday or just to let them know you love them. Surprise them with a cute floatie in their drink. I am sure it will brighten up anybody's day!

The trickiest part of this design is to make sure the texture of your meringues is not too soft. It should be able to hold up its shape, so that when you pipe on the snout and heart, it will not just sink and immediately blend into the rest of the bear. For extra tips on different textures of meringue, see Troubleshooting on page 12.

Begin by making one batch of the Basic Meringue Recipe on page 10 and make sure you have the following colors ready:

PREP THE COLORS

When mixing in the gel food coloring, try to keep the airy texture of the meringue as much as possible.

BLACK: Take 1 tablespoon (15 ml) of meringue and add 5 to 6 drops of black gel food coloring. Mix, using a small spatula or spoon. Depending on how pigmented your black food coloring is, add 2 to 3 drops extra to intensify the color, if needed. The meringue does not have to be pitch black; dark gray is good enough! Transfer to a piping bag with no piping tip.

RED: Place one-third of the remaining meringue in a mixing bowl and add 4 to 6 drops of red gel food coloring. Depending on how red you want the hearts to be, add fewer or more drops of red gel food coloring (but not more than 10 drops in total). Mix in the color, using a small spoon or spatula, and transfer to a piping bag fitted with one round piping tip #6.

BROWN: To the remaining two-thirds of the meringue, add 4 to 6 drops of brown gel food coloring to create a light brown color. You could leave it as it is, or add 1 drop of yellow gel food coloring to add more warmth to the color. Mix in the color, using a small spoon or spatula.

Divide the brown meringue between two piping bags: one-third to a piping bag fitted with the other round piping tip #6, and the remaining two-thirds of brown meringue to another piping bag fitted with round piping tip #2A.

PIPE THE BEARS

1. Preheat your oven to 160°F (70°C) and place a baking sheet on the middle rack.

2. Use the brown meringue fitted with round piping tip #2A to pipe a ball shape about 1 inch (2.5 cm) in diameter and ½ inch (1.3 cm) high onto one parchment square. Smooth out any rough edges, using a baking scriber or toothpick. Repeat this process until you have a total of four balls on the parchment square.

3. Using the brown meringue fitted with round piping tip #6, pipe two small dots per bear to create the ears and one in the middle to create the snout of each bear.

4. Use the red meringue fitted with round piping tip #6 to pipe a small heart just below the snout of each bear. Use a baking scriber or toothpick to adjust the shape, making sure to create a sharp point at the bottom of the heart.

5. Go back to the brown meringue fitted with round piping tip #6 and pipe small dots on each side of the heart to create the arms on each bear. This way, it will look as if the bear is holding the heart.

6. Take the piping bag of black meringue and make a small cut at the tip, just enough for the meringue to be pipeable. Pipe two small dots onto each bear's face to create the eyes and pipe one small dot on the top part of the snout.

7. Dip your baking scriber or toothpick into black meringue and draw a mouth onto the snout. This method works best to create fine lines.

8. After you have made four bears on the first parchment paper square, carefully transfer them to the oven, onto the baking sheet, to bake. Proceed with making the next four bears and put them straight into the oven after piping, continuing until all 16 bears are in the oven.

BAKE THE FLOATIES

9. Once all the bears are in the oven, bake them for 60 minutes. After 60 minutes, increase the oven temperature to 175°F (80°C) and bake for 30 minutes.

10. After baking the bears for 90 minutes in total, turn off the oven and let them sit in the oven for another 20 minutes to continue the drying process. Take them out of the oven and allow to cool completely.

See image on page 8.

SPOOKY HALLOWEEN PUMPKINS

→ Difficulty level: Intermediate ←
→ Yield: 12 cookies ←
about 1½ inches (4 cm) each ←

It's that spooky season again: Halloween! These Halloween-inspired floaties are spooky yet adorable. You can make the ghosts any way you like, with vampire teeth or a witch hat, or keep them as they are.

Something important about this design is the order in which you pipe certain elements. Even though there is no right or wrong way, certain techniques can help you create better shapes and details, such as adding more texture to the pumpkins and piping on the little ghosts. For all the black details of this design, we will be using black meringue and our baking scriber to draw them on. However, if you are not comfortable with that yet, feel free to use a black edible marker instead.

Begin by making one batch of the Basic Meringue Recipe on page 10 and make sure you have the following colors ready:

PREP THE COLORS

When mixing in the gel food coloring, try to keep the airy texture of the meringue as much as possible.

BLACK: You can skip making the black meringue if you'll be using an edible marker. Take 1 tablespoon (15 ml) of meringue and add a pea-sized drop of black gel food coloring. Mix in the color, using a small spoon or spatula, and transfer to a piping bag fitted with round piping tip #2.

(continued)

INGREDIENTS AND TOOLS

Black, green and orange gel food coloring

Red gel food coloring (optional)

5 piping bags

1 #2 round piping tip

1 #12 round piping tip

1 #6 round piping tip

1 #2A round piping tip

Baking sheet

6 (4-inch [10-cm]) squares parchment paper

Baking scriber or toothpicks

Black edible marker (optional)

SPOOKY HALLOWEEN PUMPKINS (CONTINUED)

GREEN: Take 1 tablespoon (15 ml) of meringue and add 3 to 5 drops of green gel food coloring, preferably using a darker green as opposed to bright green, because this will be used to create the stem and leaves. Mix in the color, using a small spoon or spatula, and transfer to a piping bag with no piping tip.

WHITE: Transfer one-third of the remaining meringue directly to a piping bag fitted with round piping tip #12. (No food coloring required.)

ORANGE: To the remaining two-thirds of the meringue, add 5 to 7 drops of orange gel food coloring. Mix in the coloring, using a spatula, and add an additional drop of red gel food coloring to intensify the color, if needed. Divide the orange meringue between two piping bags: one-third to a piping bag fitted with the round piping tip #6, and the remaining two-thirds of orange meringue to another piping bag fitted with round piping tip #2A.

PIPE THE FLOATIES

1. Preheat your oven to 160°F (70°C) and place a baking sheet on the middle rack.

2. We'll be making two pumpkins per square of parchment paper. Onto one square of parchment paper, use the orange meringue fitted with round piping tip #2A to pipe two ball shapes with a flat bottom, each about 1 inch (2.5 cm) in diameter.

3. Use the orange meringue fitted with round piping tip #6 to pipe vertical stripes on the sides of each ball. Use a baking scriber or toothpick to blend the vertical stripes together. Piping the vertical stripes onto the orange meringue ball will add extra definition to each pumpkin.

Skip steps 4, 5, 7 and 8 if using an edible black marker to draw on the details.

4. Then, using the black meringue fitted with round piping tip #2, pipe two small dots onto each pumpkin to create the eyes—one in the middle for the nose, and a line at the bottom part for the mouth.

5. Now, use a baking scriber or toothpick to adjust the shape of the black meringue. Create a spooky smile and three small triangles for the eyes and nose of each pumpkin.

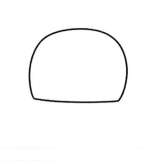

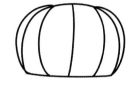

6. Then, using the white meringue fitted with round piping tip #12, pipe a ball shape on the right top part of each pumpkin. Then, pipe the "tail" of the ghost on one side. Blend both parts together, using a baking scriber. Do this for each pumpkin.

7. Back with the black meringue, pipe two small black dots onto each ghost to make the eyes. Take your baking scriber and dip it into the black meringue, then draw on the smile of the ghost right between the eyes.

8. Take a little of the white meringue, using a clean baking scriber, and carefully press it onto the eyes to create two small white dots. You can leave this part out, but I believe it makes the floaties look a lot cuter!

9. Finally, use the green meringue to pipe a stem and leaves on top of each pumpkin. Transfer your two spooky pumpkin floaties, on their parchment square, directly onto the baking sheet in the oven.

10. Repeat the above steps until all six parchment squares (12 floaties in total) are in the oven.

BAKE THE FLOATIES

11. Once all the pumpkins are in the oven, bake for 70 minutes. After 70 minutes, increase the oven temperature to 175°F (80°C) and bake for another 50 minutes.

12. After baking the pumpkins for 2 hours in total, turn off the oven and let them sit in the oven for 20 minutes to continue the drying process. Take them out of the oven and allow to cool completely.

6A

6B

8

9

HAPPY THANKSGIVING TURKEYS

Difficulty level: Advanced
Yield: 10 cookies
about 1½ inches (4 cm) each

INGREDIENTS AND TOOLS

Black, brown, green, red, yellow and orange gel food coloring

7 piping bags

1 #5 round piping tip

1 #2A round piping tip

4 #4 round piping tips

4 (6-inch [15-cm]) squares parchment paper

Baking scriber or toothpicks

It's impossible to imagine celebrating Thanksgiving without turkey on the menu—or in this case, meringue turkeys!

These turkeys are made in two stages. First, we will pipe and bake the feathers, and then we'll add the body. This creates height and shapes you could not achieve otherwise.

Begin by making one batch of the Basic Meringue Recipe on page 10 and make sure you have the following colors ready:

PREP THE COLORS

When mixing in the gel food coloring, try to keep the airy texture of the meringue as much as possible.

BLACK: Take 1 tablespoon (15 ml) of meringue and add 5 to 6 drops of black gel food coloring. Gently mix in the color, using a small spoon or spatula, and transfer to a piping bag. No piping tip is required.

BROWN: Place half of the remaining meringue in a mixing bowl and add 5 to 6 drops of brown gel food coloring. Mix in the coloring, using a small spoon or spatula, then transfer one-quarter of the brown meringue to a piping bag fitted with round piping tip #5, and the remaining three-quarters to a piping bag fitted with round piping tip #2A.

Divide the remaining meringue equally among separate mixing bowls, to make the following colors.

GREEN: To the first portion, add 3 to 4 drops of green gel food coloring and mix in the color, using a small spoon or spatula, then transfer to a piping bag fitted with one round piping tip #4.

RED: To the second portion, add 4 to 5 drops of red gel food coloring and mix in the color, using a small spoon or spatula, then transfer to another piping bag fitted with the second round piping tip #4.

YELLOW: To the third portion, add 3 to 4 drops of yellow gel food coloring and mix in the color, using a small spoon or spatula, then transfer to a separate piping bag fitted with the third round piping tip #4.

ORANGE: To the fourth portion, add 4 to 5 drops of orange gel food coloring and mix, using a small spoon or spatula, and then transfer to the final piping bag fitted with the fourth round piping tip #4.

(continued)

HAPPY THANKSGIVING TURKEYS (CONTINUED)

PIPE THE TURKEYS

1. Preheat your oven to 160°F (70°C) and place a baking sheet on the middle rack.

2. Have the following colors ready: yellow, orange, green and red. First, we are going to pipe the feathers of the turkey and bake them. Alternating the colors as you go, using one color per feather, pipe five sets of feathers onto each of two parchment squares— 10 feathers in total.

3. Transfer the feathers into the oven and bake for 40 minutes. After 40 minutes, take them out of the oven (including the baking sheet) to cool. When cooled completely, gently peel them off the parchment and set aside.

4. Place the other two parchment squares on the baking sheet to continue making the turkeys.

5. To create the body of each turkey, take the brown meringue fitted with piping tip #2A and pipe five ball shapes, about 1 inch (2.5 cm) in height, onto each parchment square, leaving about 1½ inches (4 cm) of space between the balls.

Now, take the brown meringue fitted with piping tip #5 and pipe the wings and little hairs onto each turkey.

6. Next, use the orange meringue to pipe a small beak and two feet onto each turkey.

7. Pipe a small teardrop shape right next to the beak of each turkey, using the red meringue, and adjust the shape with a baking scriber or toothpick, if needed.

8. Carefully press the feathers from earlier into the back of each turkey so they stick.

9. Finally, make a small cut at the tip of the piping bag of black meringue. Pipe two small dots next to the beak to create the eyes of the turkeys. They are ready for the oven!

BAKE THE FLOATIES

10. After you have made all 10 turkeys, transfer them, on your baking sheet, onto the middle rack of the oven. Bake them for 80 minutes, then increase the oven temperature to 175°F (80°C) and bake for 30 more minutes.

11. After baking them for 110 minutes in total, turn off the oven and let them sit in the oven for 25 minutes to continue drying. Take them out of the oven to cool completely before peeling them off the parchment.

WINTER WONDERFUL CHRISTMAS TREES

Difficulty level: Beginner
Yield: 13 to 14 cookies
about 1½ inches (4 cm) each

INGREDIENTS AND TOOLS

Yellow and green gel food coloring

2 piping bags

1 #3 round piping tip

1 #4B open star piping tip

Baking sheet

1 sheet parchment paper

Round ball sprinkles of choice

Powdered sugar

Do you enjoy Christmas baking as much as I do? Well then, I have a few cute Christmas designs coming up!

If you are new to making meringue cookies, these Christmas trees are a great beginner-level design! You can personalize them with the type of sprinkles you use and this is a fun activity to do with kids, friends or family members during the holidays. What makes them winter wonderful is that we are going to dust a little powdered sugar over them to make it look as if they have been out in the snow. You can use them to decorate your cakes or let them float in hot chocolate.

Before we get started, begin by making one batch of the Basic Meringue Recipe on page 10 and have the following colors ready:

PREP THE COLORS

When mixing in the gel food coloring, try to keep the airy texture of the meringue as much as possible.

YELLOW: Take 2 tablespoons (30 ml) of meringue and add 4 to 6 drops of yellow gel food coloring. Mix in the color, using a small spoon or spatula, and transfer to a piping bag fitted with round piping tip #3.

GREEN: To the remaining meringue, add about 3 pea-sized drops of green gel food coloring. Mix in the coloring, using a spatula. Add 2 to 3 more drops of green gel food coloring (how much you use depends on how pigmented your gel food coloring is). When the color is fully incorporated, transfer to a piping bag fitted with open star piping tip #4B.

(continued)

WINTER WONDERFUL CHRISTMAS TREES
(CONTINUED)

PIPE THE CHRISTMAS TREES

1. Line a baking sheet with parchment paper, cutting away any excess. This way, we have an even surface to work on and don't risk having lopsided Christmas trees.

2. Take your green meringue and start with the bottom of the Christmas tree. Make the base about 1½ inches (4 cm) wide. Squeeze the bag, holding it at the same spot, and then release. Hold the piping bag a little higher and squeeze again, make the middle part slightly smaller than the base, about 1 inch (2.5 cm), and release again. Finally, hold the bag a little higher and pipe the top part, about ⅝ inch (1.5 cm). Squeeze and slowly raise the bag up to create a tip. Continue to do this until you have a full baking sheet of 13 or 14 Christmas trees, leaving 1½ inches (4 cm) of space between the trees.

3. Now, let's decorate our trees! Carefully add sprinkles to the sides of the Christmas trees and use the sprinkles to create the illusion of Christmas balls.

4. Lastly, use the yellow meringue to pipe little stars on top of each Christmas tree.

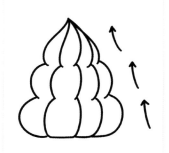

BAKE THE FLOATIES

5. Transfer the baking sheet with its Christmas trees onto the middle rack of the oven and turn on the oven to 160°F (70°C) and bake for 80 minutes.

We did not preheat the oven for this design, so the trees can slowly bake while the temperature slowly increases. This method works best when adding solid details, such as the sprinkles, onto the meringue. I've noticed when baking them in a preheated oven the details might separate from the meringue.

6. After baking the trees for 80 minutes, increase the oven temperature to 175°F (80°C) and bake for 40 more minutes.

7. After 120 minutes in total, turn the oven off and let the trees sit in the oven for 20 minutes.

8. When the trees are fully cooled, dust a small amount of powdered sugar on top of the trees to create the illusion of snow, and they are done!

CUTE CHARACTER MACARONS
and Tasty Fillings

Macarons are delicate cookies with a crisp yet chewy exterior filled with different flavorful fillings, such as buttercreams, caramels, jams and ganache.

If you follow my basic macaron recipe carefully, your macarons should not be hollow. However, making macarons requires a lot of precision, practice and patience. If it does not work out right away, try again and keep in mind that such factors as different types of ovens and environments can create different outcomes for your macarons. These factors will all be further discussed in the Troubleshooting section on page 75.

If you are new to making macarons, I would suggest starting with simpler designs, such as the Multicolored Sunset Macarons (page 111) or Lovely Valentine Hearts (page 117). These are easier to make but still look as if it took a lot of effort to make them! Once you get the hang of it, try making more intricate designs, such as Colorful Unicorns (page 103), Over the Rainbow (page 95) or one of my favorite Happy Sushi Friends (page 107)! Those will definitely be the talk of the party!

I struggled a lot when I first started making macarons, but practice really makes perfect. So, don't worry if they don't come out right the first time; just try to figure out what may have been the problem and then try again. Even if your macarons come out of the oven looking wrong, they will still be delicious!

BASIC MACARON RECIPE

Yield: 34 to 36 macaron shells

There are different methods for making macarons: the Swiss method, French method and Italian method. My personal preference is the Swiss method, which basically means heating egg whites and sugar using a double boiler, as we did for our meringue cookies!

The Swiss method makes a very strong and stable meringue, which helps prevent ending up with hollow macarons. It is also more beginner-friendly, with less chance of overmixing, compared to using the French method. Although the French method might seem easier, as it does not require heating the egg whites and sugar, that version is less stable and can be overmixed more easily, which causes hollow macarons. The Italian method also works great, but in my opinion, it requires more practice. So, the Swiss method is the best of both worlds and more foolproof for beginners!

However, keep in mind that these delicious treats can still be difficult to master as small factors can easily mess up your macarons. But don't worry! In the Troubleshooting section on page 75, I discuss some of these issues and how you can prevent them from happening again. You'll be a macaron master in no time.

All the piping tips I use for making macarons, as well as the gel food coloring, are from Wilton. You can use other brands, but the pigmentation of the food coloring may differ.

INGREDIENTS AND TOOLS

75 g almond flour

75 g powdered sugar

66 g fresh egg whites (see Troubleshooting [page 75])

60 g superfine sugar

Gel food coloring of choice

Digital food scale

Fine-mesh sieve

Stand mixer

Candy thermometer

LET'S GET STARTED

1. Measure out all of the ingredients using your digital scale—accuracy is important when making macarons. Weigh the almond flour and powdered sugar first, then transfer them to a food processor. Pulse a few times but no more than four or five times, or else your almond flour could release oils, which could lead to greasy and translucent macaron shells.

2. Using a fine-mesh sieve, sift the pulsed almond flour and powdered sugar into a bowl. This is a very important step! If you do not sift, your macarons will not have that nice, smooth top, and even though you might have very fine almond flour and powdered sugar, there still might be some lumps. Do not overfill your sieve; just fill halfway at a time, or else it will go over the sides and make a mess. Do this two times to make sure the mixture is well sifted. Discard any large particles left in the sieve.

3. Fill a pot with water to a depth of about 1 inch (2.5 cm) and bring to a simmer over medium heat.

4. In the mixing bowl of your stand mixer, combine the egg whites and superfine sugar, then place the bowl over the pot of simmering water. Make sure the bottom of the bowl is not touching the water!

5. With a spatula, stir the egg whites and superfine sugar constantly until the sugar has fully melted. Use a candy thermometer to keep an eye on the temperature of the mixture; it should not exceed 120°F (50°C). I usually remove the bowl from the heat at 113°F (45°C), as the remaining heat from the bowl will continue to melt the sugar. This process should take about 5 minutes.

6. Transfer your mixing bowl to a stand mixer and use the whisk attachment to beat the egg white mixture. Start whisking on low speed for 1 to 2 minutes, then increase to medium speed and whisk for 2 to 3 minutes, or until it becomes white and frothy.

7. Now, increase the speed to medium-high and mix until stiff peaks form. It takes me 12 to 15 minutes to form stiff peaks, but go by the consistency of your meringue and not by time! However, be careful not to overwhip the egg whites. Check your meringue by picking up the whisk; the peak should come up straight with only a slight bend at the top. Stop at this stage.

8. Add half of the sifted almond flour mixture to the meringue and stir it with a spatula. Once it is fully incorporated, add the second half and carefully mix. Make sure to scrape the sides and bottom well until you see no more streaks of almond flour or powdered sugar anymore.

(continued)

BASIC MACARON RECIPE
(CONTINUED)

9. Now you're ready to macaronage your batter and add your food coloring! Refer to the specific design you're creating to see how many colors to use, then divide the mixture into separate bowls accordingly and add the food coloring to them (but don't mix yet).

HOW TO MACARONAGE

After dividing the macaron batter into different mixing bowls and adding the gel food coloring drops, it is time to mix in the coloring to incorporate it fully and macaronage our batter until it reaches our desired consistency. Macaronage is the technique of mixing macaron batter to get rid of large air bubbles and to make it shinier and more fluid.

10. We'll be mixing one color at a time, starting with the bowl that contains the least amount of batter and working our way up to the one that contains the most. Make sure to cover the other bowls with plastic wrap, so the batter does not dry out in the meantime.

11. Add the gel food coloring and start mixing by using a spatula and spreading the macaron batter toward the sides of the bowl. Then, scrape the batter from the sides back toward the center again. Do this a few times and you will notice the batter becoming more fluid. But be careful not to overdo it, or else you might overmix it. I usually do this four to six times, but check the consistency constantly by picking up some batter with your spatula.

12. The batter is the right consistency when it flows off your spatula in a slow, consistent drizzle similar to that of honey. I like to check whether my macaron batter is ready to use by picking up some with my spatula and drawing several figure eights with the batter. The figure eights should slowly sink and blend themselves back again with the rest of the batter. This should take about 30 seconds; stop mixing at this point!

13. If the streaks are still showing after 30 seconds, you need to macaronage the batter more. If the streaks blend quickly into the rest of the batter (less than 30 seconds), it is probably slightly overmixed. So, take your time with this! You do not want undermixed batter, as this can cause lumpy or hollow macarons, but you also do not want to overmix it, as this can cause cracked or hollow macarons, or macarons with no feet. This will be discussed further in the Troubleshooting section on the next page.

14. Now that your batter has been macaronaged, you're ready to pipe your macarons! Proceed with the instructions for your chosen macaron design.

TROUBLESHOOTING

Are you having trouble baking macarons? In this section, I cover the most common mistakes when making macarons and how to solve them. Based on the outcome of your macarons, it can already tell you a lot about what went wrong!

WHY WON'T MY EGG WHITES WHIP PROPERLY?

First, are you using fresh egg whites? Very often prepackaged ones will not whip up properly. If you are having difficulties with whipping your fresh egg whites to stiff peaks, it is mostly due to grease. When whipping egg whites, make sure all of your equipment is totally grease-free. From the mixing bowl to the whisk and spatula, they all *must* be grease-free. I usually wash my equipment in hot water with a little bit of soap, then rinse well and make sure to thoroughly dry it.

Another reason might be that there are traces of egg yolk in your egg whites. When separating the egg whites from the yolk, make sure you do not have *any* yolk whatsoever in your egg whites. If this happens, you unfortunately need to start over again.

HOW CAN I CORRECTLY PIPE MY MACARONS?

Pipe your macarons at a 90-degree angle to the surface. If you pipe your macarons at a different angle, they might have uneven feet after baking.

When you finish piping a macaron, stop squeezing and pull upward in a circular motion. This is to prevent your macarons from having a pointy tip on the surface.

If you want to adjust the shape and edges of your macarons a little, that is totally fine; just use a baking scriber or toothpick to do so. However, do this immediately after piping them so they are still wet and do not form a skin in the meantime. If a skin does form and you try to adjust the shape, it will just ruin the surface of your macaron and you will not be able to achieve those nice, smooth results.

Tap your tray onto your countertop a few times while your macarons are still wet to release any large air bubbles, and adjust any gaps you see using a baking scriber or toothpick.

WHAT SURFACE IS THE BEST TO USE FOR PIPING AND BAKING MACARONS?

I personally like using parchment paper or a Teflon sheet for making my macarons. You could also pipe them directly onto a silicone mat. However, I've noticed that macarons baked on silicone need to stay a little longer in the oven, or they can stick to the mat.

Try using a baking sheet with a low rim, so when you bake the macarons, the heat can be distributed evenly.

(continued)

MY MACARONS LOOK WRONG AFTER BAKING. WHAT HAPPENED?

Baking macarons can be tricky, and there are a few common issues you might run into. I list them here, along with ways to prevent them so you can get the perfect macaron shell every time.

BROWNING MACARON SHELLS: If your macaron shells are browning in the oven, try placing their baking sheet on a lower rack in the oven or set the temperature slightly lower, between 275 to 285°F (135 to 140°C) and bake them for 2 to 3 minutes longer.

CRACKED TOP: If your macaron shells are cracking on top, you might have not rested them for long enough, your oven temperature was set too high or the baking sheet was put too close to the source of heat.

LUMPY/UNEVEN MACARONS: If your macarons are lumpy or uneven, your batter might have been undermixed or the dry ingredients may not have been properly sifted.

HOLLOW MACARONS: If your macarons are hollow inside, you might have under- or overmixed the batter, rested them for too long or your oven temperature was set too low or too high.

BUBBLED MACARON SHELLS AND (VERY) HIGH FEET: If the bottoms of your macarons (their feet) are very tall, it may be due to the meringue having been overwhipped, adding too much air to the mixture. Once you bake them, the amount of air in the shells will start to expand, making the feet very tall. Also, not tapping the baking sheet a few times before baking to release trapped air bubbles may cause bubbled macaron shells.

SOFT AND STICKY MACARON SHELLS: This might be caused by using oily almond flour (by processing it too much) or too much food coloring. Another reason might be that you overmixed the batter or underbaked the macarons.

WHAT ENVIRONMENT IS BEST FOR MAKING MACARONS?

Are you located in a very humid environment? Then, your macarons might not air-dry well. It is very crucial for your macarons to form a shell, or else they will not have feet or will crack when baking. Try to place your baking sheet with its macarons in a dry environment and do not make them when it is super humid or raining outside (with your windows open).

WHEN IS THE BEST TIME TO EAT MACARONS AND HOW LONG DO THEY KEEP?

You can eat your macarons right after you have made them (I mean, who could wait?). However, if you are patient, you can store them in an airtight container in the fridge for 24 hours for best results. The filling will slightly soften the inside of the shells, giving you that nice crispy outside but soft and chewy inside.

ROYAL ICING RECIPE

FOR DECORATING YOUR MACARONS

20 g fresh egg whites

110 g powdered sugar, divided, plus more if needed

1 tsp vanilla extract

Gel food coloring of choice

Yield: 1 cup (120 g)

Decorating macarons can be done in various ways. You could use melted chocolate, edible markers, edible paint or royal icing. Royal icing is an icing made from powdered sugar, egg whites and vanilla extract. The egg whites allow the icing to dry hard. I personally like using royal icing to decorate my macarons, since it creates a 3-D effect and texture that you cannot get when using edible markers or paint. However, it requires some practice.

This recipe creates a basic royal icing you can use to decorate your macarons. It can easily be doubled if you need more.

1. Place the egg whites in a bowl and beat, using a hand mixer, until they become frothy. This should take 2 to 3 minutes.

2. Sift the powdered sugar separately and discard any large particles. Add half (55 g) of the sifted sugar to the egg whites and use a spatula to incorporate it into the whites. Then, beat the mixture on low speed for 2 to 3 minutes. This way, you will prevent the sugar from flying everywhere.

3. Then, add the remaining 55 grams of sugar and mix on low speed until soft peaks form, which should take 3 to 5 minutes.

4. Add the vanilla and mix on low speed. The consistency you are looking for should be similar to that of toothpaste. It should be stiff enough to hold its shape, but soft enough to adjust with a baking scriber. If the mixture looks very stiff and dry, add a few drops of water; if it looks too runny, add more powdered sugar, 1 teaspoon at a time.

5. Once you are happy with the consistency, add 1 to 2 drops of gel food coloring and mix in the color. Transfer your icing to a piping bag and you are ready to decorate! Note that after decorating your macarons (or other treats), you'll want to let the royal icing dry for 20 to 30 minutes.

6. Store your leftover royal icing in an airtight food container in the fridge for up to 1 week. When you want to use it, take the royal icing out of the fridge for 30 to 45 minutes to soften it again.

You can fill your macarons with just about anything, including buttercreams, curds, jam, cream cheese, chocolate and more. The possibilities are endless, but here you'll find my five favorite fillings for the designs in this chapter. These fillings also work perfectly for cakes or cupcakes, and you could make different filling combinations as well!

CHOCOLATE HAZELNUT BUTTERCREAM
WITH A SALTED CARAMEL CORE

Chocolate Hazelnut Buttercream
Yield: 1¾ cups (410 g)

Salted Caramel
Yield: 1 cup (335 g)

This yummy buttercream is so easy to make and is always a hit! I like to pair it with my salted caramel to fill the center of my macarons, but you could use only the buttercream, if you prefer.

BUTTERCREAM

9 tbsp (125 g) unsalted butter, at room temperature

100 g powdered sugar, divided

185 g chocolate hazelnut spread, such as Nutella®, at room temperature

1 tsp vanilla extract

1 tbsp (15 ml) heavy cream

SALTED CARAMEL CORE

150 g superfine sugar

6 tbsp (85 g) unsalted butter, at room temperature, cut into 6 cubes

⅓ cup + 2 tsp (100 ml) heavy cream

About 1 tsp salt, or to taste

BUTTERCREAM

1. In a glass or metal mixing bowl, using a hand mixer, or the bowl of a stand mixer fitted with the whisk attachment, beat the butter on medium speed for 3 to 5 minutes until soft and smooth.

2. Then, add the powdered sugar 1 tablespoon (8 g) at a time. Mix on medium-low speed until the sugar is fully incorporated before adding another tablespoon (8 g) of sugar.

3. Once all the sugar is added, keep mixing on medium-low speed for 4 to 5 minutes until it has a light, creamy consistency.

4. Add the chocolate hazelnut spread, vanilla and cream, and beat on medium speed for 2 to 3 minutes. The buttercream should have a soft and creamy consistency. Transfer to a piping bag fitted with the piping tip specified in the recipe and it is ready to use!

To store the buttercream, cover it tightly and keep in the fridge for up to 1 week, or in the freezer for up to 3 months. When taking it out of the freezer, thaw the buttercream for 2 to 3 hours at room temperature, then beat for 1 to 2 minutes before using.

SALTED CARAMEL CORE

1. In a saucepan (avoid using nonstick), heat the superfine sugar over medium heat, stirring occasionally with a wooden spoon. The sugar will form clumps at first but eventually melt into a thick, dark amber-colored liquid as you continue to stir.

The sugar should be melted completely. If you notice the caramel is turning brown but the sugar has not fully melted yet, lower the heat to prevent your caramel from burning. If it starts to burn, your caramel will become bitter.

2. Once the sugar has completely melted, remove the pan from the heat and immediately add the butter, one cube at a time, stirring until the butter has fully melted before adding the next cube.

3. Once all the butter has been added and it has fully melted, return your pan to medium heat and cook again for 2 minutes, stirring occasionally.

4. Slowly add the cream but be very careful, since your caramel will bubble heavily when adding it. After all the cream has been added, stir occasionally and allow it to boil over medium heat for 6 to 8 minutes, keeping an eye on your caramel! If it looks as if it's beginning to burn, just remove the pan from the heat and keep stirring.

5. After boiling your caramel for 6 to 8 minutes, remove from the heat and add the salt. Use a wooden spoon to stir in the salt until fully incorporated and no more bubbles appear. It should turn into a glossy, smooth golden caramel.

6. Carefully transfer the caramel to a ceramic or heatproof glass bowl and allow it to cool completely. The caramel should thicken as it cools.

7. When filling your macarons, pipe a rim of the buttercream around the edge of the macaron shell, leaving the center empty. Then, transfer the caramel to a piping bag or add two scant teaspoonfuls (10 ml) of the caramel to the center of the macarons. The buttercream rim will prevent the caramel from oozing out on the sides.

You can store the caramel in an airtight container for up to 1 month in the fridge, or in the freezer for up to 3 months. When taking it out of the freezer, allow it to thaw at room temperature for 3 to 4 hours before using.

WHITE CHOCOLATE GANACHE

WITH RASPBERRY JAM

White Chocolate Ganache
Yield: 1½ cups (325 g)

Raspberry Jam
Yield: 1 cup (315 g)

This smooth white chocolate ganache only takes two ingredients to make! Because white chocolate ganache can be quite sweet and macarons are also relatively sweet on their own, I like to pair it with my raspberry jam to add some tartness.

WHITE CHOCOLATE GANACHE

250 g white chocolate, cut into chunks or in chip form

$^2/_3$ cup (160 ml) heavy cream

RASPBERRY JAM

250 g frozen raspberries

150 g gelling sugar (sugar with pectin added), Dr. Oetker® brand suggested

Juice of ½ lemon

WHITE CHOCOLATE GANACHE

1. Place the chocolate in a heatproof glass or ceramic bowl.

2. In a small saucepan, bring the cream to a boil.

3. Once the cream starts to boil, add it to the white chocolate and wiggle the bowl so all the chocolate is covered with the cream, then let sit for 1 minute, stirring occasionally with a spatula, until all the chocolate has completely melted. If you still see some chunks of chocolate that haven't been melted, pop the bowl into a microwave for 20 to 30 seconds.

4. Once your ganache looks smooth and all the chocolate has melted, refrigerate it for 30 minutes, or until it has a pasty consistency and a yellowish color.

5. Now, mix the ganache with a hand mixer for 2 to 3 minutes, or just until it turns white with a mousse-like consistency. Be careful not to overwhip, or the cream might split! If this does happen, heat the ganache in a microwave for a few seconds and stir until it becomes smooth again. Let it cool and whip again.

To store the ganache, cover it with plastic wrap, placed so it touches the surface of the ganache, and keep in an airtight container in the fridge for up to 3 days, or in the freezer for up to 1 month. Thaw by microwaving the ganache in 10-second intervals, mixing with a spatula after each interval, then beat the ganache again for 1 to 2 minutes on medium speed before using.

RASPBERRY JAM

1. In a saucepan over medium heat, heat the frozen raspberries, stirring constantly, until they have softened. This should take about 5 minutes.

2. Add all the gelling sugar and continue to stir until the raspberries have completely broken down and the pectin has dissolved.

3. Squeeze in the lemon juice and let it boil for 5 minutes over medium heat.

4. Transfer the raspberry jam directly to a Mason jar or a heatproof glass or ceramic bowl. You could strain out the seeds if you want, but I kept the seeds in mine. Refrigerate the jam for 6 to 8 hours or overnight.

5. When filling your macarons, pipe a rim of white chocolate ganache around the edge of the macaron shell, leaving the center empty, then fill the center with raspberry jam. The ganache will prevent the jam from oozing out on the sides.

Your raspberry jam will keep in the fridge in an airtight jar for up to 4 weeks, or in the freezer for up to 6 months. To thaw, simply transfer the jar from the freezer to the fridge and leave it there overnight. Once you have thawed it, do not refreeze the jam again.

CINNAMON CREAM CHEESE BUTTERCREAM

WITH APPLE CARAMEL CORE

Cinnamon Cream Cheese Buttercream
Yield: 2½ cups (560 g)

Apple Caramel Core
Yield: 1⅞ cups (425 g)

This cinnamon cream cheese filling is perfect for the fall and winter seasons. I like to pair it with my apple caramel core to add a yummy surprise in the center of my macarons, plus it goes so well with the cinnamon cream cheese flavor! You could also simply leave out the ground cinnamon to have a natural cream cheese filling.

CINNAMON CREAM CHEESE BUTTERCREAM

1. In a mixing bowl, using a hand mixer, or the bowl of a stand mixer fitted with the whisk attachment, beat the cream cheese and butter together for 2 to 3 minutes on medium speed, or until light and fluffy.

2. Reduce the mixer speed to low and add 1 tablespoon (8 g) of powdered sugar at a time.

3. Once all the sugar is well incorporated, add the cinnamon and vanilla, then increase the mixer speed to medium-high and beat for 3 to 5 minutes, or until light and fluffy. Don't mix for too long, or your buttercream might split. If that is the case, reheat it in a microwave at 10-second intervals and stir with a spatula. It should start to come back together again.

Store your cinnamon cream cheese buttercream in an airtight container for up to 5 days in the fridge.

CINNAMON CREAM CHEESE BUTTERCREAM

8 oz (250 g) cream cheese, at room temperature

9 tbsp (125 g) unsalted butter, at room temperature

175 g powdered sugar, divided

10 g ground cinnamon, or to taste

1 tsp vanilla extract

APPLE CARAMEL CORE

1 Granny Smith apple, peeled, cored and diced into scant ¼-inch (6-mm) cubes

175 g superfine sugar

4 tsp (20 ml) water

⅓ cup + 2 tsp (90 ml) heavy cream

6 tbsp + 1 tsp (90 g) unsalted butter, diced into 6 cubes

Sea salt (optional; I used about 5 g)

APPLE CARAMEL CORE

1. In a medium-sized saucepan, combine the apple cubes, superfine sugar and water. Heat over medium-low heat for 4 to 5 minutes, stirring with a wooden spatula, until all the sugar has dissolved.

2. Cook for 5 to 7 minutes without stirring until the sugar turns into golden amber-colored caramel.

3. Remove the pan from the heat and carefully add the cream. It will start to bubble heavily but don't worry; this will slowly stop as you keep stirring.

4. Place the pan back over low heat and add the butter, one cube at a time. Make sure the butter is fully melted before adding the next one and keep stirring until all the butter is incorporated.

5. Turn off the heat and add the sea salt (if using). Keep stirring until well combined.

6. Transfer to a ceramic or heatproof glass bowl and chill in the fridge for 6 to 8 hours or overnight.

7. When filling your macarons, pipe a rim of cinnamon cream cheese buttercream around the edge of the macaron shell, leaving the center empty. Add two scant teaspoonfuls (10 ml) of the apple caramel to the center of the macarons. The cinnamon cream cheese buttercream will prevent the caramel from oozing out on the sides.

Store the apple caramel in an airtight container for up to 1 week in the fridge, or up to 2 months in the freezer. When taking it out of the freezer, allow it to thaw at room temperature for 3 to 4 hours before using. Once the caramel has been thawed, do not refreeze it.

COOKIES AND CREAM BUTTERCREAM

Yield: 1²/₃ cups (375 g)

Who doesn't love cookies and cream? This super-easy buttercream tastes amazing on macarons, cakes or cupcakes, or just on its own. All you need is a basic buttercream recipe and pulverized chocolate sandwich cookies, such as Oreo®. You could also use other cookies, such as Biscoff®, KitKat® or peanut butter cookies for this recipe.

INGREDIENTS

8 chocolate sandwich cookies, such as Oreos

9 tbsp (125 g) unsalted butter, at room temperature

150 g powdered sugar, divided

1 tsp vanilla extract

2 tsp (10 ml) heavy cream (optional)

1. Pulverize the cookies (with their filling) in a food processor or crush them finely in a ziplock bag by using a pan or rolling pin. Set them aside.

2. In a mixing bowl, using a hand mixer, or the bowl of a stand mixer fitted with the whisk attachment, beat the butter for 4 to 5 minutes on medium speed, or until light and fluffy.

3. Reduce the mixer speed to low and add 1 tablespoon (8 g) of powdered sugar at a time. Once all the sugar is well incorporated, add the vanilla and cream, increase the mixer speed to medium-high and beat for 4 to 5 minutes.

4. Add the crushed cookies and mix on low speed for 1 minute, or until well incorporated.

5. When you're ready to pipe the buttercream, make sure to use a large, open piping tip so the pieces of cookie do not get stuck in the piping tip.

Cover tightly and store in the fridge for up to 1 week, or in the freezer for up to 2 months. When taking out of the fridge, thaw the buttercream at room temperature for 1 hour and beat it again for 1 to 2 minutes before using. When taking out of the freezer, thaw the buttercream in the fridge overnight, then for 1 hour at room temperature and beat it for 1 to 2 minutes before using.

ZESTY LEMON BUTTERCREAM

Yield: 1⅜ cups (315 g)

INGREDIENTS

10 tbsp (150 g) unsalted butter, at room temperature

150 g powdered sugar, divided

Zest of 2 lemons

Juice of ½ lemon

If you don't like fillings that are too sweet, this is the perfect filling to use for your macarons. It is made with fresh lemon juice and lemon zest, which makes it tangy but also fragrant. I like to pair this filling with spring- and summer-themed macarons.

1. In a mixing bowl, using a hand mixer, or the bowl of a stand mixer fitted with the whisk attachment, beat the butter for 3 to 4 minutes on medium speed, or until light and fluffy.

2. Reduce the mixer speed to low and add 1 tablespoon (8 g) of powdered sugar at a time. Once all the sugar is well incorporated, mix on medium speed for 3 to 4 minutes.

3. Add the lemon zest and mix on medium speed for 1 minute. Adding lemon zest really gives the buttercream a nice lemon flavor, whereas the lemon juice is added for sharpness.

4. Reduce the mixer speed to medium-low and slowly add the lemon juice. Once all the lemon juice is added, increase the speed to medium-high and mix for 2 minutes. The lemon juice should be fully incorporated and the buttercream should be smooth and creamy.

Store the lemon buttercream in an airtight container for up to 2 weeks in the fridge, or 3 months in the freezer. When stored in the fridge, thaw the lemon buttercream at room temperature for 1 hour and beat it again for 1 to 2 minutes before using. When stored in the freezer, thaw the lemon buttercream in the fridge overnight, then for 1 hour at room temperature and beat it for 1 to 2 minutes before using.

CUTEST BREAKFAST

LOVELY AVOCADO, TASTY TOAST AND SUNNY-SIDE UP EGGS

Difficulty level: Intermediate
Yield: 28 macaron shells
(8 avocados, 10 toasts, 10 eggs)

Waking up to these cute breakfast macarons will brighten up anybody's day! For this recipe, we are going to create three different designs of macarons for a full breakfast. You can make them as a set or individually. I would also suggest using a different filling for each design! I have divided the breakfast into separate components, so you will exactly know which equipment or colors you need for each design.

I used royal icing for decorating my macarons, but to make it more beginner-friendly, you could use an edible black marker or edible paint instead to draw on the final details. However, I do highly suggest using royal icing, as it gives the eyes a glossier and even cuter finish.

Before we get started, make sure you have the following ready:

Begin by making one batch of the Basic Macaron Recipe on page 72. When the almond flour and powdered sugar are sifted into the meringue, mix the ingredients together with a spatula until there's no visible trace of dry almond flour or powdered sugar anymore. Now, we are going to divide our macaron batter to color it.

PREP THE COLORS

Divide the macaron batter into three equal portions, one for each design (if making all three designs).

(continued)

LOVELY AVOCADO

Green and brown gel food coloring

3 piping bags

1 #6 round piping tip

1 #12 round piping tip

1 #10 round piping tip

TASTY TOAST

Brown and yellow gel food coloring

2 piping bags

1 #6 round piping tip

1 #12 round piping tip

SUNNY-SIDE UP EGGS

Yellow, orange and white gel food coloring

2 piping bags

1 #12 round piping tip

1 #8 round piping tip

Baking sheet

Parchment paper

Cutest Breakfast templates (page 182)

Baking scriber or toothpicks

Royal icing (page 77)

Black and pink gel food coloring, for royal icing

3 piping bags, for royal icing

3 #2 round piping tips, for royal icing

1 batch filling of your choice (I used Zesty Lemon Buttercream [page 85])

CUTEST BREAKFAST

(CONTINUED)

LOVELY AVOCADO

DARK GREEN: Place one-quarter of the first portion in a mixing bowl and add 5 to 6 drops of green gel food coloring. Mix in the color, using a spatula, until you have the desired consistency. It should slowly flow off your spatula in a thick and steady drizzle (like honey). Transfer the batter to a piping bag fitted with round piping tip #6.

BROWN: Place another one-quarter of the first portion in a separate mixing bowl and add 4 to 5 drops of brown gel food coloring. Mix in the color, using a spatula, until you have the desired consistency. It should slowly flow off your spatula in a thick and steady drizzle (like honey). Transfer the batter to a piping bag fitted with round piping tip #12.

LIGHT GREEN: To the remaining one-half of the first portion, add 3 to 4 drops of green gel food coloring. Mix in the color until you have the desired consistency. Transfer to a piping bag fitted with round piping tip #10.

TASTY TOAST

BROWN: Place one-third of the second portion in a mixing bowl and add 3 drops of brown gel food coloring and 1 drop of yellow gel food coloring. Mix in the color, using a spatula, until you have the desired consistency. It should slowly flow off your spatula in a thick and steady drizzle (like honey). Transfer the batter to a piping bag fitted with round piping tip #6.

LIGHT BROWN/BEIGE: To the remaining two-thirds of the second portion, add 2 drops of brown gel food coloring and 1 drop of yellow gel food coloring. Mix in the color, using a spatula, until you have the desired consistency. It should slowly flow off your spatula in a thick and steady drizzle (like honey). Transfer the batter to a piping bag fitted with round piping tip #12.

SUNNY-SIDE UP EGGS

YELLOW/ORANGE: Place one-third of the third portion in a mixing bowl. Add 3 drops of yellow gel food coloring and 1 to 2 drops of orange gel food coloring. Mix in the color, using a spatula, until you have the desired consistency. It should slowly flow off your spatula in a thick and steady drizzle (like honey). Transfer the batter to a piping bag fitted with round piping tip #12.

WHITE: To the remaining two-thirds of the third portion, add 4 to 5 drops of white gel food coloring. Mix in the color, using a spatula, until you have the desired consistency. It should slowly flow off your spatula in a thick and steady drizzle (like honey). Transfer the batter to a piping bag fitted with round piping tip #8.

PIPE THE DESIGN

1. Line your baking sheet with parchment paper, cutting away any excess. There are three templates for this set of macarons. Slip the appropriate template between the parchment paper and the baking sheet to help you pipe uniform shapes. If your parchment paper keeps moving, put some batter underneath each corner to hold the sheet steady.

2. On the illustrations, you will see numbers 1 through 3; that is the order of piping the colors. If you need to adjust the shape or edges, use a baking scriber or toothpick, but do this immediately while they're still wet!

LOVELY AVOCADO

3. Start by using the dark green macaron batter fitted with round piping tip #6 to fill in all of the avocado outlines (number 1 of the template).

4. Then, use the light green macaron batter fitted with round piping tip #10 to fill in all the avocados' interiors (number 2), leaving the heart part open.

5. Finally, use the brown macaron batter fitted with round piping tip #12 to fill in all the heart-shaped avocado pits (number 3). Once you're done, carefully remove the template and tap your baking sheet a few times to remove any large air bubbles, and smooth out any gaps on your macarons, using a toothpick or baking scriber.

TASTY TOAST

6. Start by using the brown macaron batter fitted with round piping tip #6 to fill in section number 1, the outline of the toast for all the macarons.

7. After you've piped the outline for all the macarons, use the light brown/beige macaron batter fitted with round piping tip #12 to fill in the rest of the toast (section number 2). Once you're done, carefully remove the template and tap your baking sheet a few times to remove any large air bubbles, and smooth out any gaps on your macarons, using a toothpick or baking scriber.

SUNNY-SIDE UP EGGS

8. Use the white macaron batter fitted with round piping tip #8 to fill in all the egg whites (number 1).

9. After you've piped all the egg whites, use the yellow/orange macaron batter fitted with round piping tip #12 to fill in all the yolks (number 2). Once you're done, carefully remove the template and tap your baking sheet a few times to remove any large air bubbles, and smooth out any gaps on your macarons, using a baking scriber or toothpick.

BAKE AND ASSEMBLE

10. Once you are done piping all the macarons, allow them to air-dry for 1 to 1½ hours. The surface of the macarons should be completely dry to the touch. In the meantime, preheat the oven to 300°F (150°C).

11. Once the macarons are finished resting, bake them for 13 to 15 minutes on the middle rack. If you touch the top of a macaron, it should not feel soft. If it does, you may need to give them a little more time in the oven. When your macarons are done, allow them to cool completely before peeling off the parchment.

(continued)

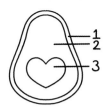

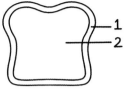

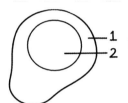

12. While your macarons bake, color your royal icing. Place one-half of the royal icing in a mixing bowl and add 4 to 5 drops of black gel food coloring. Mix in the coloring, using a spoon or spatula, and transfer to a piping bag fitted with one round piping tip #2.

13. In a separate mixing bowl, color one-quarter of the remaining royal icing pink by adding 1 drop of pink gel food coloring. Mix in the color and transfer to a separate piping bag fitted with another round piping tip #2.

14. Transfer the remaining one-quarter of the royal icing directly to a piping bag fitted with the final round piping tip #2.

15. Decorate one macaron shell at a time. Only decorate half of the macaron shells so that you have a front and back side (shell) for each macaron. Use the black icing to pipe the eyes and mouth, and the white icing to add small dots onto the eyes to create that glossy look; then, finally, use pink icing to make the blushing cheeks.

16. Let the royal icing dry on the macarons for 20 to 30 minutes before adding the buttercream filling. Then, take a macaron shell, turn it upside down so the flat surface faces upward and fill the entire surface with the buttercream. The filling should be the same height as the macaron shell. Top off with another macaron shell with the flat side on the filling and press slightly to form a sandwich. Repeat with all the shells, and your cute breakfast macarons are done!

15A

15B

15C

COOL ICE CREAM CONES

Difficulty level: Advanced
Yield: 26 to 28 macaron shells

INGREDIENTS AND TOOLS

Light beige, brown and pink gel food coloring

Yellow gel food coloring (optional)

4 piping bags (1 for the royal icing)

1 #10 round piping tip

2 #8 round piping tips

Baking sheet

Parchment paper

Cool Ice Cream Cones template (page 185)

Baking scriber or toothpicks

Sprinkles of choice

Royal icing (page 77)

1 #2 round piping tip

1 batch filling of your choice (I used White Chocolate Ganache [page 80])

We all love ice cream, especially on a hot day. Luckily, you don't have to worry about these macarons, as they will not melt. They are small enough for you to eat more than one. I filled these with my White Chocolate Ganache with Raspberry Jam filling (page 80), so the flavor matches the design.

The trickiest part about these macarons is their shape and the amount of detail. We are going to pipe the shapes first, then decorate them with sprinkles and finish them off by adding royal icing details. If you are new to making macarons, I would suggest you try an easier shape, such as oval popsicles. Use real popsicle sticks to make them look even more real! They are less difficult to make but are just as cute as these ice cream cones. However, if you are up for the challenge, let's get started!

Make sure you have the following ready:

Begin by making one batch of the Basic Macaron Recipe on page 72. When the almond flour and powdered sugar are sifted into the meringue, mix the ingredients together with a spatula until there's no visible trace of dry almond flour or powdered sugar anymore. Now, we are going to divide our macaron batter to color it.

PREP THE COLORS

Divide the macaron batter equally among three separate mixing bowls to make the following colors.

LIGHT BEIGE: To the first portion, add 3 to 4 drops of light beige food coloring and 1 drop of brown gel food coloring. If you don't have light beige, you could add 2 drops of brown gel food coloring and 1 drop of yellow gel food coloring to create a similar color for the ice cream cone. Mix in the color, using a spatula, until you have the desired consistency. It should slowly flow off your spatula in a thick and steady drizzle (like honey). Transfer the batter to a piping bag fitted with round piping tip #10.

PINK: To the second portion, add 4 to 5 drops of pink gel food coloring. Mix in the color, using a spatula, until you have the desired consistency. It should slowly flow off your spatula in a thick and steady drizzle (like honey). Transfer the batter to a piping bag fitted with one round piping tip #8.

(continued)

COOL ICE CREAM CONES (CONTINUED)

BROWN: To the third portion, add 5 to 6 drops of brown gel food coloring. Mix in the color, using a spatula, until you have the desired consistency. It should slowly flow off your spatula in a thick and steady drizzle (like honey). Transfer the batter to a piping bag fitted with the other round piping tip #8.

PIPE THE DESIGN

1. Line a baking sheet with parchment paper, cutting away any excess. Slip the template between the parchment paper and baking sheet to help you pipe uniform shapes. If your parchment paper keeps moving, put some batter underneath each corner to hold the sheet steady.

2. On the illustrations, you will see numbers 1 through 3; that is the order of piping the colors. Working one macaron at a time, start off by using the light beige macaron batter fitted with round piping tip #10 to fill in the cone (number 1).

3. Then, use the pink macaron batter fitted with one round piping tip #8 to pipe the ice cream (number 2). Use a baking scriber to adjust the shape, if needed. Make sure to do this immediately after piping, so the batter is still wet.

4. Now, use the brown macaron batter fitted with round piping tip #8 to pipe on the chocolate (number 3).

5. Repeat steps 1 through 4 until you have a full baking sheet of ice cream macarons. Once you are done, tap your baking sheet a few times to remove any large air bubbles and smooth out any gaps, using a baking scriber or toothpick.

6. Add some sprinkles to the chocolate part (number 3) of the macarons while they're still wet!

BAKE AND ASSEMBLE

7. Allow your macarons to air-dry for 1½ to 2 hours. Shaped macarons need more resting than round macarons. The surface of the macarons should be completely dry to the touch. In the meantime, preheat the oven to 300°F (150°C).

8. Once the macarons are finished resting, bake them for 15 to 17 minutes on the middle rack. If you touch the top of a macaron, it should not feel soft. If it does, you may need to give them a little more time in the oven. When your macarons are done, allow them to cool completely before peeling off the parchment.

9. Meanwhile, get your royal icing ready. Take 2 tablespoons (16 g) of the icing, mix in the light beige gel food coloring and transfer to a piping bag fitted with round piping tip #2.

10. Pipe a waffle pattern onto the cone part of the macarons and let them air-dry for 20 to 30 minutes, or until dry.

11. Take one macaron shell, turn it upside down so the flat surface faces upward and add a dollop of white chocolate ganache. Top off with another macaron shell with the flat side on top of the filling and press slightly to form a sandwich. The filling should have the same height as a macaron shell. Repeat with all the remaining shells and your cute ice cream cone macarons are done!

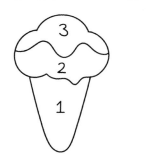

OVER THE RAINBOW

→ Difficulty level: Advanced ←
→ Yield: 22 to 24 macaron shells ←

These colorful macarons are sure to brighten anyone's day. Make them for St. Patrick's Day, Pride Day or for any other special occasion.

I filled these rainbow macarons with cream cheese buttercream, using the filling recipe on page 82 but leaving out the ground cinnamon. What makes these rainbow macarons advanced is their shape and the number of steps and colors you have to make. Also, be aware that shaped macarons need more resting time than regular round macarons. These rainbow macarons might take some effort, but they will be all worth it!

Make sure you have the following ready:

INGREDIENTS AND TOOLS

White, red, yellow, green, blue and orange gel food coloring

6 piping bags

1 #12 round piping tip

4 #6 round piping tips

1 #7 round piping tip

Baking sheet

Parchment paper

Over the Rainbow template (page 186)

Baking scriber or toothpicks

Black edible marker or black edible paint

1 batch Cinnamon Cream Cheese Buttercream, omitting the cinnamon (page 82)

Begin by making one batch of the Basic Macaron Recipe on page 72. When the almond flour and powdered sugar are sifted into the meringue, mix the ingredients together with a spatula until there's no visible trace of dry almond flour or powdered sugar anymore. Now, we are going to divide our macaron batter to color it.

PREP THE COLORS

WHITE: Place one-third of the macaron batter in a mixing bowl and add 5 to 6 drops of white gel food coloring. Mix in the color, using a spatula, until you have the desired consistency. It should slowly flow off your spatula in a thick and steady drizzle (like honey). Transfer the batter to a piping bag fitted with round piping tip #12.

Divide the remaining macaron batter into five equal portions to make the following colors.

RED: To the first portion, add 3 to 4 drops of red gel food coloring. Mix in the color, using a spatula, until you have the desired consistency. It should slowly flow off your spatula in a thick and steady drizzle (like honey). Transfer it to a piping bag fitted with the first round piping tip #6.

YELLOW: To the second portion, add 3 to 4 drops of yellow gel food coloring. Mix in the color, using a spatula, until you have the desired consistency. It should slowly flow off your spatula in a thick and steady drizzle (like honey). Transfer it to a piping bag fitted with the second round piping tip #6.

GREEN: To the third portion, add 3 to 4 drops of green gel food coloring. Mix in the color, using a spatula, until you have the desired consistency. It should slowly flow off your spatula in a thick and steady drizzle (like honey). Transfer it to a piping bag fitted with the third round piping tip #6.

BLUE: To the fourth portion, add 3 to 4 drops of blue gel food coloring. Mix in the color, using a spatula, until you have the desired consistency. It should slowly flow off your spatula in a thick and steady drizzle (like honey). Transfer it to a piping bag fitted with the fourth round piping tip #6.

(continued)

ORANGE: To the fifth portion, add 2 drops of orange gel food coloring and 3 drops of yellow gel food coloring. Mix in the color, using a spatula, until you have the desired consistency. It should slowly flow off your spatula in a thick and steady drizzle (like honey). Transfer it to a piping bag fitted with round piping tip #7.

PIPE THE DESIGN

1. Line a baking sheet with parchment paper, cutting away any excess. Slip the template between the parchment paper and baking sheet to help you pipe uniform shapes. If your parchment paper keeps moving, put some batter underneath each corner to hold the sheet steady.

2. Start by piping all the sun rays for all the macarons, using the orange macaron batter. Make about 15 macaron shells with the sun (these will be the front sides of your macarons, and the 15 shells without the suns will be the back sides).

3. Once all the sun rays are piped, use the same orange macaron batter to pipe the middle part of all the suns.

4. Now, make the rainbows. Pipe them starting from the bottom toward the top. So, start with blue, then green, then yellow and finally red. Repeat until you have a full baking pan of rainbows.

5. Finish by using white macaron batter to pipe all the clouds. Then, carefully remove the template and tap your baking sheet a few times to remove any large air bubbles, and smooth out any gaps on your macarons, using a baking scriber or toothpick.

BAKE AND DECORATE

6. After all the macarons have been piped, allow them to air-dry for 1½ to 2 hours. The surface of the macarons should be completely dry to the touch. In the meantime, preheat the oven to 300°F (150°C).

7. Once the macarons have dried, bake them for 14 to 17 minutes on the middle rack. If you touch the top of a macaron, it should not feel soft. If it does, they may need a little more time in the oven. Cool completely before peeling off the parchment and decorating them.

8. Use black edible marker or edible paint to draw the eyes and mouths on the suns and clouds. You will only have to draw them onto the front side (the shells with the sun).

9. Once the details have fully dried, take one macaron shell (back side of the rainbow), turn it upside down so the flat surface faces upward and fill the entire surface with cream cheese buttercream. Top off with another macaron shell (front side of the rainbow) with the flat side on top of the filling and press slightly to form a sandwich. The filling should have the same height as a macaron shell. Repeat with all the shells and you're done!

3

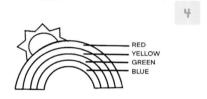

4

RED
YELLOW
GREEN
BLUE

5

8

STUNNING SEASHELLS

WITH EDIBLE PEARLS

Difficulty level: Intermediate
Yield: 26 to 28 macaron shells

I made these seashell macarons the first time for a friend's daughter's mermaid-themed birthday party. They were one of my first with a complex shape, and it took some practice to get them right. However, after making them a few times, I was finally happy with the outcome and I will explain the technique that made all the difference!

I used white chocolate pearls for my seashell macarons, but you could use sugar pearls or make your own using marzipan or fondant. You could also leave the macaron shells as they are, but I highly recommend brushing them with edible pearl luster dust to give them that luminescent glow.

Before we get started, make sure you have the following ready:

INGREDIENTS AND TOOLS

Blue and violet or purple gel food coloring

2 piping bags

1 #5 round piping tip

1 #12 round piping tip

Parchment paper

Baking sheet

Stunning Seashells template (page 187)

Baking scriber or toothpicks

Kitchen gloves

Small soft paintbrush

Edible pearl luster dust

Chocolate pearls (white)

1 batch filling of your choice (I used Zesty Lemon Buttercream [page 85])

Begin by making one batch of the Basic Macaron Recipe on page 72. When the almond flour and powdered sugar are sifted into the meringue, mix the ingredients together with a spatula until there's no visible trace of dry almond flour or powdered sugar anymore.

PREP THE COLOR

To the entire batch of the macaron batter, add 3 drops of blue gel food coloring and 1 drop of violet or purple gel food coloring. We are going for a light blue color with a hint of purple for the seashells.

Mix the ingredients until you're happy with the consistency. It should slowly flow off your spatula in a thick and steady drizzle (like honey).

Transfer one-quarter of the macaron batter to a piping bag fitted with round piping tip #5 and the remaining three-quarters of the macaron batter to a piping bag fitted with round piping tip #12.

(continued)

STUNNING SEASHELLS
(CONTINUED)

PIPE THE MACARONS

1. Line a baking sheet with parchment paper, cutting away any excess. Slip the template between the parchment paper and baking sheet to help you pipe uniform shapes. If your parchment paper keeps moving, put some batter underneath each corner to hold the sheet steady.

2. On the illustrations, you'll see numbers 1 through 3. The order of piping the seashells is very important! Pipe section number 1 first. Start off at the top, squeeze and slowly drag downward to create that teardrop shape. Repeat this step for the entire baking sheet of macarons.

3. Once you are done piping section number 1, let the macarons sit for 5 minutes before proceeding to section number 2. This lets the batter dry slightly before you move on, giving you much more visible lines on the seashells. If you were to pipe section numbers 1 and 2 right away, the batter would just blend together. After 5 minutes, pipe section number 2 for each macaron on the baking sheet.

4. Finally, use the other piping bag fitted with round piping tip #5 to pipe the base of the shells (number 3 on the illustration).

5. When all the shells are done, carefully remove the template and tap your baking sheet a few times to remove any large air bubbles and smooth out any gaps on your macarons, using a baking scriber or toothpick.

BAKE AND ASSEMBLE

6. Allow your macarons to air-dry for 1½ hours. The surface of the macarons should be completely dry to the touch. In the meantime, preheat the oven to 300°F (150°C).

7. Once the macarons are finished resting, bake them for 15 to 18 minutes on the middle rack. If you touch the top of a macaron it should not feel soft. If it does, you may need to give them a little more time in the oven. Allow them to cool completely before peeling off the parchment.

8. Take a clean, soft paintbrush and brush edible pearl luster dust over the macaron shells. It is best to do this wearing kitchen gloves, and over parchment paper to catch any excess powder.

9. To assemble and fill each macaron, take one macaron shell and turn it upside down so the flat surface faces upward and pipe small pea-sized dots

of the lemon buttercream onto the macaron shell. Add a little more filling toward the front of the macaron shell and add the white chocolate pearl.

10. Top off with another macaron shell with the flat side on top of the filling and slightly pinch the ends together to form a seashell. Repeat with all the remaining shells and they are done!

SLEEPY PANDAS

Difficulty level: Intermediate
Yield: 24 to 26 macaron shells

These panda macarons are so cute; you almost just want to keep them instead of eating them. The great thing about making macarons is that they are very versatile. If you are new to them, I would suggest you only make the head of the panda and leave out the body part; but if you are up for a challenge, try it out! The template for these cute panda macarons can be found on page 188. You can fill them with any filling you like, but I filled mine using my Cookies and Cream Buttercream on page 84 to stick with the black-and-white theme.

Make sure you have the following ready:

INGREDIENTS AND TOOLS

White or violet gel food coloring (optional)

Black gel food coloring

4 piping bags

1 #2 round piping tip

1 #10 round piping tip

1 #3 round piping tip

1 #7 round piping tip

Baking sheet

Parchment paper

Sleepy Pandas template (page 188)

Baking scriber or toothpicks

1 batch filling of your choice (I used Cookies and Cream Buttercream [page 84])

Begin by making one batch of the Basic Macaron Recipe on page 72. When the almond flour and powdered sugar are sifted into the meringue, mix the ingredients together with a spatula until there's no visible trace of dry almond flour or powdered sugar anymore. Now, we are going to divide our macaron batter to color it.

PREP THE COLORS

Divide the macaron batter equally between two mixing bowls to make the following colors.

WHITE: If you do not have white or violet gel food coloring, you can leave this batter as it is. However, keep in mind that your macarons will come out slightly light beige after baking due to the almond flour.

But if you do have white or violet gel food coloring, to the first portion of macaron batter, add 5 to 6 drops of white gel food coloring or use a toothpick and dip just the tip in violet gel food coloring and add this to the batter. Violet cancels out any yellow tones, making the batter whiter. Just be careful not to add too much, or your batter will turn purple.

Use a spatula to mix in the coloring. When the batter slowly flows off your spatula in a thick and steady drizzle (like honey), stop mixing at this point!

Transfer 1 tablespoon (15 ml) of the white macaron batter to a piping bag fitted with round piping tip #2, and the remaining white macaron batter to a piping bag fitted with round piping tip #10.

BLACK: To the second portion, add 4 to 6 drops of black gel food coloring and mix it in by folding your macaron batter until you've reached the desired consistency. When the batter slowly flows off your spatula in a thick and steady drizzle (like honey), stop mixing at this point!

Transfer 1 tablespoon (15 ml) of the black macaron batter to a piping bag fitted with round piping tip #3, and the remaining black batter to another piping bag fitted with round piping tip #7.

(continued)

SLEEPY PANDAS
(CONTINUED)

PIPE THE DESIGN

1. Line a baking sheet with parchment paper, cutting away any excess. Slip the template between the parchment paper and baking sheet to help you pipe uniform shapes. If your parchment paper keeps moving, put some batter underneath each corner to hold the sheet steady.

2. On the illustrations, you will see numbers 1 through 3; that is the order of piping the colors. So, use the black macaron batter fitted with piping tip #7 to pipe all the feet, arms and ears of all the pandas first (number 1).

3. Then, use the white macaron batter fitted with piping tip #10 to pipe all the bodies and heads of the pandas (number 2). Adjust the shape a little, using a baking scriber. Do this immediately after piping so the batter is still wet. If you do this later, it would just ruin the surface of your macarons. See page 75 for more tips on troubleshooting.

4. Go back to the same black macaron batter fitted with piping tip #7, and onto the templates showing the front portions of the panda, pipe the eyes of all the pandas (number 3). For the templates showing the back portions of the panda, pipe on the tails.

5. Take the other piping bag of black macaron batter fitted with round piping tip #3 and, on the templates showing the front portions of the panda, pipe on the nose of all the pandas.

6. Lastly, take white macaron batter fitted with round piping tip #2, and on the templates showing the front portions of the panda, pipe two lines for the eyes and we're done!

BAKE AND ASSEMBLE

7. After making all the pandas, carefully remove the template and tap your baking sheet a few times to remove any large air bubbles and smooth out any gaps on your macarons, using a baking scriber or toothpick.

8. Allow your macarons to air-dry for 1½ to 2 hours. The surface of the macarons should be completely dry to the touch. In the meantime, preheat the oven to 300°F (150°C).

9. Once the macarons are finished resting, bake them for 15 to 17 minutes on the middle rack. If you touch the top of a macaron, it should not feel soft. If it does, you may need to give them a little more time in the oven. When your macarons are done, allow them to cool completely before peeling off the parchment.

10. Take a macaron shell (the back side of the panda), turn it upside down so the flat surface faces upward and fill the entire surface with cookies and cream buttercream. Top off with another macaron shell (the front side of the panda) with the flat side on top of the filling and press slightly to form a sandwich. The filling should have the same height as a macaron shell. Repeat with all the shells and your cute panda macarons are done!

COLORFUL UNICORNS

Difficulty level: Advanced
Yield: 26 to 28 macaron shells

From cakes to cupcakes to macarons, unicorns have always been a trend when it comes to baking. In this recipe, I will show you my version of unicorn macarons. All the colors are made with macaron batter, except for the horns and facial features. I used edible gold paint for the horns and a black edible marker to make the eyes and mouths.

To really showcase the beautiful bright colors of these unicorn macarons, I filled them with my White Chocolate Ganache (page 80). You can also add Raspberry Jam (page 81) or Salted Caramel (page 79) in the center, so there is a nice surprise when you bite into them.

Before we get started, make sure you have the following ready:

INGREDIENTS AND TOOLS

White, blue, yellow and pink gel food coloring

Violet gel food coloring (optional)

5 piping bags

1 #6 round piping tip

1 #12 round piping tip

3 #8 round piping tips

Baking sheet

Parchment paper

Colorful Unicorns template (page 189)

Baking scriber or toothpicks

Gold edible paint

Small soft paintbrush

Black edible marker

1 batch filling of your choice (I used White Chocolate Ganache with Raspberry Jam [page 80])

Begin by making one batch of the Basic Macaron Recipe on page 72. When the almond flour and powdered sugar are sifted into the meringue, mix the ingredients together with a spatula until there's no visible trace of dry almond flour or powdered sugar anymore. Now, we are going to divide our macaron batter to color it.

PREP THE COLORS

WHITE: Place one-half of the macaron batter in a mixing bowl and add 5 to 6 drops of white gel food coloring. You could also add a tiny amount of violet color to cancel out the yellow tones but be *very* careful not to add too much (just the tip of a toothpick is enough).

Mix in the color, using a spatula, until you reach the desired consistency. It should slowly flow off your spatula in a thick and steady drizzle (like honey). Transfer one-quarter of the macaron batter to a piping bag fitted with round piping tip #6 and the other three-quarters of the macaron batter to a piping bag fitted with round piping tip #12.

Divide the remaining macaron batter equally among three separate mixing bowls to make the following colors.

(continued)

COLORFUL UNICORNS (CONTINUED)

BLUE: To the first portion, add 3 to 4 drops of blue gel food coloring. Mix with a spatula until you have the desired consistency. It should slowly flow off your spatula in a thick and steady drizzle (like honey). Transfer it to a piping bag fitted with the first round piping tip #8.

YELLOW: To the second portion, add 3 to 4 drops of yellow gel food coloring. Mix with a spatula until you have the desired consistency. It should slowly flow off your spatula in a thick and steady drizzle (like honey). Transfer it to a piping bag fitted with the second round piping tip #8.

PINK: To the third portion, add 3 to 4 drops of pink gel food coloring. Mix with a spatula until you have the desired consistency. It should slowly flow off your spatula in a thick and steady drizzle (like honey). Transfer it to a piping bag fitted with the third round piping tip #8.

PIPE THE DESIGN

1. Line a baking sheet with parchment paper, cutting away any excess. Slip the template between the parchment paper and baking sheet to help you pipe uniform shapes. If your parchment paper keeps moving, put some batter underneath each corner to hold the sheet steady.

2. On the illustration, you will see numbers 1 through 5. Pipe section number 1 (part of the unicorn's mane), using the blue macaron batter fitted with round piping tip #8. Do this for all 26 macarons before moving on to step 3.

3. Then, pipe section number 2 (part of the unicorn's mane), using the yellow macaron batter fitted with round piping tip #8, followed by section number 3 using pink macaron batter fitted with round piping tip #8. Do this for all 26 macarons.

4. Once all the manes are done, use the white macaron batter fitted with round piping tip #12 to pipe all the heads of the unicorns (number 4).

5. Then, use the other piping bag with white macaron batter fitted with round piping tip #6 to pipe all the unicorns' ears and horns (number 5).

6. Lastly, use the pink macaron batter to pipe a little swirl on top of the head (number 6).

7. After piping all the unicorns, carefully remove the template and tap your baking sheet a few times to remove any large air bubbles and smooth out any gaps on your macarons, using a baking scriber or toothpick.

(continued)

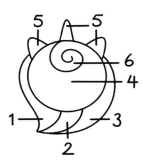

COLORFUL UNICORNS (CONTINUED)

BAKE AND DECORATE

8. Allow your macarons to air-dry for 1½ to 2 hours. The surface of the macarons should be completely dry to the touch. In the meantime, preheat the oven to 300°F (150°C).

9. Once the macarons are finished resting, bake them for 15 to 18 minutes on the middle rack. If you touch the top of a macaron, it should not feel soft. If it does, you may need to give them a little more time in the oven. When the macarons are done, allow them to cool completely before peeling off the parchment and decorating them.

10. Use a small soft paintbrush and edible gold paint to color the horn of each unicorn. Then, use an edible black marker to draw the eyes and mouth and let it dry before adding the filling.

11. Take a macaron shell (the back side of the unicorn) and fill around the edges of the macaron shell with white chocolate ganache, leaving the middle part empty. The filling should have the same height as a macaron shell. Use two small teaspoons (10 ml) to add the raspberry jam into the center of the macaron shell and top off with another macaron shell (the front side of the unicorn) to form a sandwich. Repeat with all the shells, and your macarons are done!

10

HAPPY SUSHI FRIENDS

(TWO STYLES)

Difficulty level: Advanced
Yield: 24 to 26 macaron shells

I have to admit, I probably can have sushi every day of the week. I love it so much that I even decided to make these adorable sushi macarons. The ones I made are salmon nigiri and tamago nigiri (which is a rolled layered omelet). Using a white colored filling for these macarons makes it look like it is part of the sushi rice.

I used royal icing to make the eyes and an edible black marker for the mouth. I prefer using royal icing if I want to create cute glossy eyes and edible markers if I need to draw thin lines. If you want, you can complete the final look by adding store-bought matcha buttercream and melted dark chocolate on the side to make it look like wasabi and soy sauce.

Make sure you have the following ready:

Begin by making one batch of the Basic Macaron Recipe on page 72. When the almond flour and powdered sugar are sifted into the meringue, mix the ingredients together with a spatula until there's no visible trace of dry almond flour or powdered sugar anymore. Now, we are going to divide our macaron batter to color it.

PREP THE COLORS

BLACK: Place one-fifth of the macaron batter in a mixing bowl and add 3 to 5 drops of black gel food coloring. Mix in the color, using a spatula, until you have the desired consistency. It should slowly flow off your spatula in a thick and steady drizzle (like honey). Transfer it to a piping bag fitted with round piping tip #6.

(continued)

MACARONS

Black, white, orange and yellow gel food coloring

6 piping bags

1 #6 round piping tip

1 #12 round piping tip

2 #5 round piping tips

2 #8 round piping tips

Baking sheet

Parchment paper

Happy Sushi Friends templates (page 190)

Baking scriber or toothpicks

1 batch filling of your choice (I used Cinnamon Cream Cheese Buttercream [page 82])

ICING

Royal Icing (page 77)

Black gel food coloring

2 piping bags

2 #2 round piping tips

Black edible marker

HAPPY SUSHI FRIENDS
(CONTINUED)

WHITE: Place one-half of the remaining macaron batter in a separate mixing bowl and add 5 to 6 drops of white gel food coloring. Mix in the color, using a spatula, until you have the desired consistency. It should slowly flow off your spatula in a thick and steady drizzle (like honey). Transfer the batter to a piping bag fitted with round piping tip #12.

Divide the remaining macaron batter equally between two mixing bowls to make the following colors.

ORANGE: To one portion, add 2 to 3 drops of orange gel food coloring and mix in the color, using a spatula, until you have the desired consistency. It should slowly flow off your spatula in a thick and steady drizzle (like honey). Transfer one-third of the orange macaron batter to a piping bag fitted with round piping tip #5 and the remaining two-thirds to a piping bag fitted with round piping tip #8.

YELLOW: To the second portion, add 3 to 4 drops of yellow gel food coloring and mix in the color, using a spatula, until you have the desired consistency. It should slowly flow off your spatula in a thick and steady drizzle (like honey). Transfer one-third of the yellow macaron batter to a piping bag fitted with round piping tip #5 and the remaining two-thirds to a piping bag fitted with round piping tip #8.

PIPE THE DESIGN

There are two templates for this set of macarons. You can make both or one of them.

Line a baking sheet with parchment paper, cutting away any excess. Slip each template between the parchment paper and baking sheet to help you pipe uniform shapes. If your parchment paper keeps moving, put some batter underneath each corner to hold the sheet steady.

TAMAGO NIGIRI

1. The illustration is labeled with numbers 1 through 4, which is the order of piping the colors. If you need to adjust the shape or edges as you work, use a baking scriber or toothpick and do this immediately while the batter is still wet!

2. Start by using white macaron batter fitted with round piping tip #12 to fill in number 1. Pipe this section of each macaron onto your prepared baking sheet before moving on to the next section.

3. Use the yellow macaron batter fitted with round piping tip #8 to fill in section number 2 for each macaron and let this part dry for 5 minutes before proceeding.

4. Then, use the yellow macaron batter fitted with round piping tip #5 to fill in section number 3 for each macaron.

5. Lastly, use black macaron batter to fill in section number 4 for each macaron. Once you're done, carefully remove the template and tap your baking sheet a few times to remove any large air bubbles and smooth out any gaps on your macarons, using a baking scriber or toothpick.

(continued)

HAPPY SUSHI FRIENDS

(CONTINUED)

SALMON NIGIRI

6. Start by using the white macaron batter fitted with round piping tip #12 to fill in number 1. Pipe this section of each macaron on your prepared baking sheet before moving on to the next section.

7. Then, use the orange macaron batter fitted with round piping tip #8 to fill in number 2 for each macaron and let this part dry for 5 minutes before proceeding.

8. Lastly, use the orange macaron batter fitted with round piping tip #5 to fill in part number 3 for each macaron. The stripes on top of the salmon will be made with royal icing after baking. Once you're done, carefully remove the template and tap your baking sheet a few times to remove any large air bubbles, and smooth out any gaps on your macarons, using a baking scriber or toothpick.

BAKE AND ASSEMBLE

9. After you have piped all the macarons, allow them to air-dry for 1½ hours. The surface of the macarons should be completely dry to the touch. In the meantime, preheat the oven to 300°F (150°C).

10. Once the macarons are finished resting, bake them for 14 to 16 minutes on the middle rack. If you touch the top of a macaron, it should not feel soft. If it does, you may need to give them a little more time in the oven. When the macarons are done, allow them to cool completely before peeling off the parchment and decorating them.

11. Next, color your royal icing. Take 1 tablespoon (8 g) of icing and add 2 drops of black gel food coloring. Mix and transfer to a piping bag fitted with round piping tip #2. Use this to make the eyes. Note the two designs: one for opened eyes and one for closed eyes.

12. Take 2 tablespoons (16 g) of white royal icing and transfer it directly to a piping bag fitted with round piping tip #2. Use this to make the stripes on the salmon and to make the small white dots on the eyes.

13. Use a black edible marker to draw on the smiles and let air-dry for 20 to 30 minutes, or until completely dry.

14. Take a macaron shell (the back side of the sushi), turn it upside down so the flat surface faces upward and fill the entire surface with cinnamon cream cheese filling. Top off with another macaron shell (the front side of the sushi) with the flat side on top of the filling and press slightly to form a sandwich. The filling should have the same height as a macaron shell. Repeat with all the shells and they're done!

MULTICOLORED SUNSET MACARONS

Difficulty level: Beginner
Yield: 26 to 28 macaron shells

These dreamy sunset macarons look as if they are difficult to make, yet you will be surprised at how easy it actually is! The fun part is that you can use any colors you like. You could go for pastel colors to make spring- and Easter-inspired macarons, or dark colors, such as black, purple and blue, and spray some glitter on top to make galaxy-themed macarons. The possibilities are endless!

For this particular recipe, we are going to go for a summer sunset theme. I filled them with my Zesty Lemon Buttercream (page 85), as I wanted a nice white filling to showcase the beautiful colors of these macarons.

Before we get started, make sure you have the following ready:

INGREDIENTS AND TOOLS

Red, orange and yellow gel food coloring

Plastic wrap

1 piping bag

1 #2A round piping tip

Baking sheet

Parchment paper

Multicolored Sunset template (page 192)

Baking scriber or toothpicks

1 batch filling of your choice (I used Zesty Lemon Buttercream [page 85])

Begin by making one batch of the Basic Macaron Recipe on page 72. When the almond flour and powdered sugar are sifted into the meringue, mix the ingredients together with a spatula until there's no visible trace of dry almond flour or powdered sugar anymore. Now, we are going to divide our macaron batter to color it.

PREP THE COLORS

Divide your macaron batter equally among three different mixing bowls.

RED: To the first portion, add 4 to 5 drops of red gel food coloring. Mix in the coloring, using a spatula, until you have the desired consistency. It should slowly flow off your spatula in a thick and steady drizzle (like honey). Stop mixing at this point and set aside.

ORANGE: To the second portion, add 4 to 5 drops of orange gel food coloring. Mix in the coloring, using a spatula, until you have the desired consistency. It should slowly flow off your spatula in a thick and steady drizzle (like honey). Stop mixing at this point and set aside.

YELLOW: To the third portion, add 4 to 5 drops of yellow gel food coloring. Mix in the coloring, using a spatula, until you have the desired consistency. It should slowly flow off your spatula in a thick and steady drizzle (like honey). Stop mixing at this point and set aside.

(continued)

MULTICOLORED SUNSET MACARONS
(CONTINUED)

PIPE THE MACARONS

1. Take a sheet of plastic wrap and spread it over your kitchen counter. Place the colored macaron batter in horizontal lines across the plastic wrap in this order: red, orange and yellow.

2. Once you have done that, take both ends of the plastic wrap and roll it up to form a sausage. Cut off any excess plastic on the sides.

3. Carefully transfer the colored sausage (with the plastic wrap) to a piping bag fitted with round piping tip #2A.

4. Line a baking sheet with parchment paper, cutting away any excess. Slip the template between the parchment paper and baking sheet to help you pipe uniform shapes.

5. When piping the macarons, keep the tip in the middle of the template and squeeze the bag. When the template is filled, stop squeezing and make a small swirl at the end. Repeat until you have piped a full baking sheet of macarons.

6. Once you're done, carefully remove the template and tap your baking sheet a few times to remove any large air bubbles, and smooth out any gaps on your macarons, using a baking scriber or toothpick.

BAKE THE MACARONS

7. Allow your macarons to air-dry for 1 to 1½ hours. The surface of the macarons should be completely dry to the touch. In the meantime, preheat the oven to 300°F (150°C).

8. Once the macarons are finished resting, bake them for 15 to 17 minutes on the middle rack. When your macarons are done, allow them to cool completely before peeling off the parchment and adding the filling.

9. Take one macaron shell, turn it upside down so the flat surface faces upward and fill the entire surface with the lemon buttercream. Top off with another macaron shell with the flat side on top of the filling and press slightly to form a sandwich. The filling should have the same height as a macaron shell. Repeat with all the shells and your macarons are done!

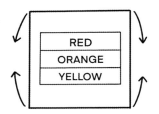

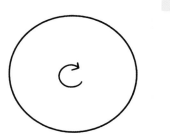

CHEERFUL EASTER EGGS

Difficulty level: Beginner
Yield: 26 to 28 macaron shells

Celebrate Easter with these cute macarons. You can decorate these Easter eggs however you like, which also makes this a fun activity to do with kids.

You can use edible markers, edible paint or royal icing to decorate. If you are planning on doing this with kids, I would suggest you use edible markers and edible paint instead of royal icing since they're a bit easier to work with. However, I do want to show how beautifully you can decorate these simple Easter eggs by using royal icing. Make sure your icing is not too thin, or else you will not be able to make those intricate details. You can find my royal icing recipe on page 77, which also includes tips on how to thicken the icing.

Before we get started, make sure you have the following ready:

MACARONS

Pink and yellow gel food coloring

2 piping bags

2 #2A round piping tips

Baking sheet

Parchment paper

Cheerful Easter Eggs template (page 193)

Baking scriber or toothpicks

1 batch filling of your choice (I used Chocolate Hazelnut Buttercream [page 78])

ICING

Royal icing (page 77)

Blue and purple gel food coloring

3 piping bags

3 round #2 piping tips

Begin by making one batch of the Basic Macaron Recipe on page 72. When the almond flour and powdered sugar are sifted into the meringue, mix the ingredients together with a spatula until there's no visible traces of dry almond flour or powdered sugar anymore. Now, divide the macaron batter equally between two mixing bowls.

PREP THE COLORS

PINK: To one portion, add 3 to 4 drops of pink gel food coloring. Mix in the coloring, using a spatula, until you have the desired consistency. It should slowly flow off your spatula in a thick and steady drizzle (like honey). Stop mixing at this point and transfer the batter to a piping bag fitted with one round piping tip #2A.

YELLOW: To the remaining portion, add 3 to 4 drops of yellow gel food coloring. Mix in the coloring, using a spatula, until you have the desired consistency. It should slowly flow off your spatula in a thick and steady drizzle (like honey). Stop mixing at this point and transfer the batter to a piping bag fitted with the other round piping tip #2A.

(continued)

CHEERFUL EASTER EGGS
(CONTINUED)

PIPE THE MACARONS

1. Line a baking sheet with parchment paper, cutting away any excess. Slip the template between the parchment paper and baking sheet to help you pipe uniform shapes. If your parchment paper keeps moving, put some batter underneath each corner to hold the sheet steady.

2. On the design, you'll see numbers 1 and 2. Ignore the patterns of the step-by-step illustrations and pipe oval-shaped macarons: use the pink macaron batter to fill in number 1, and the yellow macaron batter to fill in number 2.

3. After piping all the macarons, carefully remove the template and tap your baking sheet a few times to remove any large air bubbles and smooth out any gaps on your macarons, using a baking scriber or toothpick.

BAKE AND DECORATE

4. Allow your macarons to air-dry for 1 to 1½ hours. The surface of the macarons should be completely dry to the touch. In the meantime, preheat the oven to 300°F (150°C).

5. Once the macarons are finished resting, bake them for 14 to 16 minutes on the middle rack. When your macarons are done, allow them to cool completely before peeling off the parchment and icing them.

6. Next, prepare the royal icing colors:

WHITE: Transfer one-third of the royal icing to a piping bag fitted with round piping tip #2 (no food coloring required).

Divide the remaining icing equally between two separate mixing bowls.

BLUE: To one portion, add 1 drop of blue gel food coloring. Mix in the color, using a spoon or spatula, and transfer to a piping bag fitted with one round piping tip #2.

LILAC/PURPLE: To the second portion, add 1 drop of purple gel food coloring. Mix in the color, using a spoon or spatula, and transfer to a piping bag fitted with the other round piping tip #2.

7. Now, it's time to decorate! You can recreate one of the patterns of the step-by-step illustrations or pipe your own fun pattern onto the Easter egg macarons. Once you're done decorating them, let them air-dry for 20 to 30 minutes, or until the royal icing has set.

8. Take one macaron shell, turn it upside down so the flat surface faces upward and fill the entire surface with the chocolate hazelnut buttercream. Top off with another macaron shell with the flat side on top of the filling and press slightly to form a sandwich. The filling should have the same height as a macaron shell. Repeat with all the shells and your Easter egg macarons are done!

7A

7B

LOVELY VALENTINE HEARTS

Difficulty level: Beginner
Yield: 24 to 26 macaron shells

These heart-shaped macarons are a great treat for almost any occasion! You could make them to surprise a loved one on either Valentine's Day or a special anniversary.

These macarons were one of the first nonround designs I made. I baked them for Valentine's Day for my friends and they all loved them! To stick with the Valentine theme, I filled them with my Chocolate Hazelnut Buttercream and Raspberry Jam filling that you can find on pages 78 and 81.

Make sure you have the following ready:

INGREDIENTS AND TOOLS

Red gel food coloring

1 piping bag

1 #2A round piping tip

Baking sheet

Parchment paper

Lovely Valentine Hearts template (page 194)

Baking scriber or toothpicks

1 batch Chocolate Hazelnut Buttercream and Raspberry Jam (pages 78 and 81)

Begin by making one batch of the Basic Macaron Recipe on page 72. When the almond flour and powdered sugar are sifted into the meringue, mix the ingredients together with a spatula until there's no visible trace of dry almond flour or powdered sugar anymore.

PREP THE COLOR

To the entire batch of macaron batter, add 4 to 6 drops of red gel food coloring and continue to mix until the color is fully incorporated. Add an additional 2 to 3 drops of red gel food coloring if you want a brighter red color.

Keep folding your macaron batter until it has the right consistency. It should slowly flow off your spatula in a thick and steady drizzle (like honey). Stop mixing at this point!

PIPE THE DESIGN

1. Transfer the macaron batter to a piping bag fitted with round tip #2A. Line a baking sheet with parchment paper, cutting away any excess. Slip the template between the parchment paper and baking sheet to help you pipe uniform shapes. If your parchment paper keeps moving, put some batter underneath each corner to hold the sheet steady.

(continued)

LOVELY VALENTINE HEARTS

(CONTINUED)

2. For each heart, begin by piping at the top left and pull down toward the bottom center. Then, pipe at the top right and pull down toward the bottom center.

3. Use a baking scriber or toothpick to adjust the shape a little, if needed. Do this immediately after piping, or else your macarons will form a skin and you will not get smooth results.

4. Repeat steps 2 and 3 until you have a full baking sheet of heart-shaped macarons.

5. Carefully remove the template and tap your baking sheet a few times to remove any large air bubbles and smooth out any gaps on your macarons, using a baking scriber or toothpick.

BAKE AND ASSEMBLE

6. Allow your macarons to air-dry for 1 to 1½ hours. The surface of the macarons should be completely dry to the touch. In the meantime, preheat the oven to 300°F (150°C).

7. Once the macarons are finished resting, bake them for 14 to 16 minutes on the middle rack. When your macarons are done, allow them to cool completely before peeling off the parchment.

8. Take one macaron shell, turn it upside down so the flat surface faces upward and pipe around the edges with the chocolate hazelnut buttercream leaving the middle part empty. Use a scant teaspoonful to fill the middle part with raspberry jam, making sure not to overfill the center, so the jelly does not come out on the sides.

9. Finally, top off with another macaron shell with the flat side on top of the filling and press slightly to form a sandwich. Repeat with all the shells.

2A

2B

5

SUMMER WATERMELON

Difficulty level: Beginner
Yield: 22 to 24 macaron shells

Getting excited for the summer? Try making these watermelon macarons! They look intricate but are actually quite easy to make. I filled them with my Zesty Lemon Buttercream (page 85) as I found the tanginess of the filling suitable for these macarons, but you can use any filling you'd like!

As you may have noticed, I added black sesame seeds to the ingredients list. We will be using them as the seeds of our watermelon macarons. You can find them in most Asian grocery stores, or skip them and use a black edible marker instead.

Before we get started, make sure you have the following ready:

INGREDIENTS AND TOOLS

Red and green gel food coloring

3 piping bags

1 #10 round piping tip

1 #4 round piping tip

1 #5 round piping tip

Baking sheet

Parchment paper

Summer Watermelon template (page 195)

Baking scriber or toothpicks

Black edible marker or black sesame seeds

1 batch filling of your choice (I used Zesty Lemon Buttercream [page 85])

Begin by making one batch of the Basic Macaron Recipe on page 72. When the almond flour and powdered sugar are sifted into the meringue, mix the ingredients together with a spatula until there's no visible trace of dry almond flour or powdered sugar anymore. Now, we are going to divide our macaron batter to color it.

PREP THE COLORS

RED/DARK PINK: Place one-half of the macaron batter in a mixing bowl and add 5 to 7 drops of red gel food coloring. Mix in the color, using a spatula, until you have the desired consistency. It should slowly flow off your spatula in a thick and steady drizzle (like honey). Stop mixing at this point! Transfer the red macaron batter to a piping bag fitted with round piping tip #10.

Divide the remaining macaron batter equally between two separate mixing bowls to make the following colors.

LIGHT GREEN: To one portion, add 3 to 4 drops of green gel food coloring. Mix the color, using a spatula, until you have the desired consistency. It should slowly flow off your spatula in a thick and steady drizzle (like honey). Transfer the batter to a piping bag fitted with round piping tip #4.

DARK GREEN: To the second portion, add 5 to 6 drops of green gel food coloring and carefully mix in the color, using a spatula, until you have the desired consistency. It should slowly flow off your spatula in a thick and steady drizzle (like honey). Transfer the batter to a piping bag fitted with round piping tip #5.

(continued)

SUMMER WATERMELON
(CONTINUED)

PIPE THE DESIGN

1. Line a baking sheet with parchment paper, cutting away any excess. Slip the template between the parchment paper and baking sheet to help you pipe uniform shapes.

2. On the illustration, you see numbers 1 through 3; that is the order of piping the colors. Use the dark green macaron batter first to fill in the outer rim of the watermelon (number 1) for all the macarons.

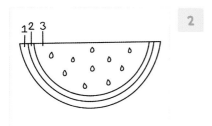

3. Once you're done with piping all the outer rims, use the light green macaron batter to fill in the inner rims of the watermelons (number 2).

4. Finally, use red macaron batter to fill in the interior of the watermelon (number 3), and use a baking scriber or toothpick to adjust or sharpen the edges. Do this immediately while they're still wet!

5. There are two options to create the seeds. You can either bake the macarons now and draw on the seeds, using a black edible marker afterward, *or* add the black sesame seeds now while the macarons are still wet.

6. After you are done piping all the watermelons, carefully remove the template and tap your baking sheet a few times to remove any large air bubbles and smooth out any gaps on your macarons, using a baking scriber or toothpick.

BAKE THE MACARONS

7. Allow your macarons to air-dry for 1 to 1½ hours. The surface of the macarons should be completely dry to the touch. In the meantime, preheat the oven to 300°F (150°C).

8. Once the macarons are finished resting, bake them for 14 to 16 minutes on the middle rack. When your macarons are done, allow them to cool completely before peeling off the parchment.

9. Take one macaron shell, turn it upside down so the flat surface faces upward and fill the entire surface with the lemon buttercream. Top off with another macaron shell with the flat side on top of the filling and slightly press to form a sandwich. The filling should have the same height as a macaron shell. Repeat with all the shells and your watermelon macarons are done!

WINTER WONDERLAND BUNNIES

→ Difficulty level: Advanced ←
→ Yield: 22 to 24 macaron shells ←

I love winter, especially when it comes to baking! Just adding a scarf, earmuffs or a beanie to your creations makes them instantly adorable! I made these winter-inspired bunny macarons, but you could also leave off the scarf and earmuffs to make regular bunny macarons.

To stick with the seasonal theme, I filled these bunnies with my Cinnamon Cream Cheese Buttercream with Apple Caramel Core (page 82).

Make sure you have the following ready:

INGREDIENTS AND TOOLS

Blue, red and white gel food coloring

Violet gel food coloring (optional)

4 piping bags

2 #7 round piping tips

1 #10 round piping tip

1 #2A round piping tip

Baking sheet

Parchment paper

Winter Wonderland Bunnies template (page 196)

Baking scriber or toothpicks

1 batch Cinnamon Cream Cheese Buttercream with Apple Caramel Core (page 82)

Begin by making one batch of the Basic Macaron Recipe on page 72. When the almond flour and powdered sugar are sifted into the meringue, mix the ingredients together with a spatula until there's no visible trace of dry almond flour or powdered sugar anymore. Now, we are going to divide our macaron batter to color it.

PREP THE COLORS

BLUE: Place one-quarter of the macaron batter in a mixing bowl and add 3 to 4 drops of blue gel food coloring. Mix in the color, using a spatula, until you have the desired consistency. It should slowly flow off your spatula in a thick and steady drizzle (like honey). Transfer to a piping bag fitted with one round piping tip #7.

RED: Place another one-quarter (an equal amount to the blue) of the macaron batter in a separate mixing bowl and add 4 to 5 drops of red gel food coloring. Mix in the color, using a spatula, until you have the desired consistency. It should slowly flow off your spatula in a thick and steady drizzle (like honey). Stop mixing at this point and transfer the batter to a piping bag fitted with round piping tip #10.

WHITE: To the remaining macaron batter, add 4 to 6 drops of white gel food coloring to make your batter. You could also add a *very* small amount (just the tip of a toothpick) of violet color into your macaron batter, but be very careful not to add too much, or else it'll turn purple. You could also leave your macaron batter as it is, but just keep in mind the bunny macarons will turn out light beige after baking.

(continued)

WINTER WONDERLAND BUNNIES

(CONTINUED)

Carefully mix in the color, using a spatula, until you have the desired consistency—it should slowly flow off your spatula in a thick and steady drizzle (like honey). Transfer one-third of the macaron batter to a piping bag fitted with the second round piping tip #7 and the other two-thirds of the macaron batter to another piping bag fitted with round piping tip #2A.

PIPE THE DESIGN

1. Line a baking sheet with parchment paper, cutting away any excess. Slip the template between the parchment paper and baking sheet to help you pipe uniform shapes. If your parchment paper keeps moving, put some batter underneath each corner to hold the sheet steady.

2. On the illustration, you will see numbers 1 through 5. Start by piping all the scarves (number 1) by using the red macaron batter.

3. After piping all the scarves, use the white macaron batter fitted with round piping tip #2A to fill in all the heads of the bunnies (number 2).

4. Next, pipe all the earmuffs (number 3) using the blue batter.

5. Then, fill in all the ears of the bunnies (number 4) by using the white macaron batter fitted with round piping tip #7.

6. Lastly, go back to using the red macaron batter, to fill in number 5, the rest of the scarf. The reason we're piping the scarf in two stages is to add dimension. If you were to pipe numbers 1 and 5 at the same time, it would just blend the two parts together.

7. After piping all the bunnies, carefully remove the template and tap your baking sheet a few times to remove any large air bubbles and smooth out any gaps on your macarons, using a baking scriber or toothpick. Be aware that the ones without earmuffs are the back side of the macarons!

BAKE AND DECORATE

8. Allow your macarons to air-dry for 1½ to 2 hours. The surface of the macarons should be completely dry to the touch. In the meantime, preheat the oven to 300°F (150°C).

9. Once the macarons are finished resting, bake them for 15 to 18 minutes on the middle rack. If you touch the top of a macaron, it should not feel soft. If it does, you may need to give them a little more time in the oven. Let the macarons cool completely before peeling off the parchment.

10. Use edible markers or edible paint to draw on the eyes and nose, and let these features dry before adding the filling.

11. Take a macaron shell (the back side of the bunny), turn it upside down so the flat surface faces upward and fill around the edges with cream cheese buttercream, leaving the middle empty. The filling should have the same height as a macaron shell. Place a scant teaspoonful of the apple caramel into the center of the macaron shell and top off with another macaron shell (the front side of the bunny) with the flat side on top of the filling and press slightly to form a sandwich. Repeat with all the shells and your cute macarons are done!

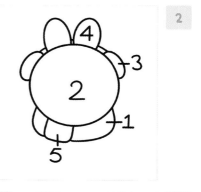

SQUISHY MARSHMALLOWS

and Hot Chocolate Surprises

You won't believe how fun it is to make marshmallows, especially if you can make them in any shape you like, such as lovely dinosaurs (page 133), cute cat paws (page 135), adorable sea turtles (page 139) and so on!

The idea of making marshmallows never came to my mind until I started posting meringue cookie videos on TikTok and Instagram. A lot of people were confused and asked whether they were marshmallows or meringue cookies. So, I thought, *Why not try making marshmallows to show people the difference between the two?*

Marshmallows are soft, squishy and do not require any baking. Meringue cookies, on the other hand, are hard, crunchy and do need to be baked in the oven. I am absolutely obsessed with corgis and especially their cute fluffy butts. So, the first marshmallows I ever made were corgi butts! I was instantly hooked, and I am sure you will be as well!

In general, marshmallows do not have any flavor; this is why we add vanilla extract to the recipe. However, you could basically add any flavored extract of your choice, such as almond, strawberry, banana, cinnamon, mint and more.

BASIC MARSHMALLOW RECIPE

Yield: 16 marshmallows 2 inches (5 cm) each

INGREDIENTS AND TOOLS

30 g fresh egg whites

45 g superfine sugar, divided

2 gelatin sheets

2 tsp (10 ml) light corn syrup

1 tsp vanilla extract or other flavored extract

Cornstarch, for dusting

Digital food scale

Hand mixer

Candy thermometer

Making marshmallows can be a difficult task, as it sets *very* fast. The consistency is also very important! If it is too liquid, you will not be able to pipe details, as it will not hold its shape. If it is too thick and difficult to pipe, most likely the mixture has already set. But don't worry—I'll walk you through each step to make the process easier!

For all the marshmallow recipes, *no* piping tip is required, which is a good thing—since the mixture sets very quickly, we often need to soften it again, and my preferred way to do this is by popping it (including the piping bag) into the microwave for a few seconds. Some people prefer to put the piping bags in warm water, but I find that water can get into the bag. More tips and tricks will be further discussed in the Troubleshooting section (page 130).

The gel food coloring I use in my marshmallow designs is from the Wilton brand. You can use other brands, but keep in mind the pigmentation of the food coloring may differ. This recipe can be doubled if you'd like to make even more marshmallows.

HOW TO MAKE IT

1. In a clean glass or metal mixing bowl, combine the egg whites and 15 grams of the superfine sugar.

2. Use a hand mixer to mix the ingredients together on medium-high speed for 5 to 7 minutes, or until stiff peaks form. Set this mixture aside. I do not use a stand mixer for making marshmallows because we are working with very small quantities and hot sugar syrup. The hot sugar syrup sinks toward the bottom of the bowl and often cannot be mixed properly with a stand mixer, unlike with a hand mixer.

3. Fill a bowl with 1 inch (2.5 cm) of cold water and put both gelatin sheets into the water, making sure they are completely covered. Set aside for the gelatin to soften.

4. In a small saucepan, combine the remaining 30 grams of superfine sugar, the corn syrup and 8 to 10 drops of water. Heat the sugar mixture over medium heat without stirring until bubbles start to appear. Insert a candy thermometer and heat the sugar mixture to 240°F (115°C), then remove the pan from the heat.

5. Working quickly, transfer the sugar mixture immediately to the stiffly beaten egg whites and mix for 2 to 3 minutes, or until the ingredients are all well combined. If you do not work fast enough, you will not be able to achieve that smooth texture, as the sugar mixture will start to set.

6. Remove the gelatin sheets from the cold water—they should be soft by now—and squeeze out any excess water. Transfer the soft gelatin sheets to a small, microwave-safe bowl and heat them in a microwave on the lowest power setting for 13 to 16 seconds, or until fully melted.

7. Working quickly again, add the melted gelatin to the egg whites along with the vanilla and mix with a hand mixer for 2 minutes. If you do not work fast enough, you will not be able to achieve that smooth texture, as the gelatin will start to set and will not properly mix into the egg whites. The consistency of your marshmallow mixture should look just like meringue. If it looks too runny and soft, keep mixing until it starts to thicken. Once you are happy with the consistency, stop mixing.

Your basic marshmallow recipe is now done! Now, follow the rest of the instructions for the marshmallow design of your choosing.

5

2A

6

2B

7A

4

7B

TROUBLESHOOTING

In this section, I will cover the most common problems and mistakes with making marshmallows and how you can fix them. I also added an alternative recipe in case you can't seem to get your hands on gelatin sheets. Remember, it takes a little practice to make character marshmallows, but once you get the hang of it, you'll be hooked!

OH, NO! MY MARSHMALLOW MIXTURE HAS SET TOO EARLY, WHAT NOW?

Be aware that the marshmallow mixture sets *very* fast. To bring back the soft consistency, transfer the marshmallow mixture to a glass or ceramic bowl and microwave for 2 to 3 seconds (in intervals, if needed) to soften your mixture again. If it is already in a piping bag, put the piping bag with marshmallow mixture into the microwave. Between intervals (never while the microwave is heating), use a spatula to stir the mixture or massage the piping bag using your hands. Microwave for no longer than 2 to 3 seconds at a time, or else you might overheat and cook the egg whites. If this happens, unfortunately you cannot use it anymore and must start over.

WHY IS THE CONSISTENCY SO IMPORTANT FOR MAKING MARSHMALLOWS?

Being sure you have the right consistency might actually be the hardest thing about making marshmallows. At first, I struggled with this and tried out all kinds of different textures to find what works best for each result I was going after.

If you need to create height or if the marshmallow needs to hold its shape properly, the mixture should not be too soft. So, if you need to heat it in a microwave, keep a very close eye on it and, when removing it from the microwave, stir with a spatula or massage the mixture with your hands to check the consistency. If it is a little too soft, just wait a few minutes and check again. I prefer to pipe a small amount onto a plate or other flat surface to check the consistency of my marshmallow mixture first before using it.

If you need to blend colors or certain elements together, it is better to work with a softer consistency. That way, it will still be easily adjustable with a baking scriber and the surface will set smooth. If the marshmallow mixture is starting to set and you try adjusting it with a baking scriber afterward, it will only mess up the surface and you won't be able to achieve nice, smooth results.

MY MARSHMALLOWS LOOKED FINE WHEN THEY WERE DONE BUT ARE NOW BECOMING STICKY. WHAT'S HAPPENING?

Your environment might be the cause of it. If it is hot and humid, your marshmallows will absorb moisture from the air, causing the stickiness. Sift cornstarch over your marshmallows until they are fully covered. Let them sit in the cornstarch for 1 hour before dusting the remainder off and transferring them to an airtight container. Brush a little extra cornstarch on them to really make sure they won't stick to one another.

Another reason might be that the mixture you worked with was too runny and liquid to begin with, because your marshmallow mixture was still hot when transferred into piping bags or was not mixed long enough. In both cases, your mixture will contain too much liquid. At first when you start using it, it might look just fine, but if you let it sit for some time or a few days, you will notice the colors bleeding into one another and your marshmallows becoming sticky. So, make sure you do not undermix it!

Also, avoid using liquid food coloring and only use gel food coloring to color your marshmallow mixture. This helps minimize the amount of moisture in your marshmallow mixture.

CAN I REPLACE OR LEAVE OUT THE CORN SYRUP?

Yes! The main reason that corn syrup is added is to prevent crystallization of the sugar. It is not necessary, but it keeps the marshmallows soft and adds chewiness to them. So you can either leave out the corn syrup or replace it with an equal quantity of golden syrup, agave syrup or honey. Golden syrup is my preferred substitution as it has the same chemical properties. Honey and agave syrup will also work but won't prevent crystallization as well as corn syrup or golden syrup.

CAN I REPLACE OR LEAVE OUT THE GELATIN SHEETS?

You can replace the gelatin sheets with powdered gelatin, but don't just swap it out in my Basic Marshmallow Recipe (page 128). Instead, assemble the following ingredients:

- *10 g (225-bloom) unflavored powdered gelatin, such as Knox® brand*
- *²/₃ cup (160 ml) water, divided*
- *35 g egg whites*
- *200 g superfine sugar*
- *4 tsp (20 g) light corn syrup*
- *1 tsp vanilla extract*

Then, begin by blooming the gelatin first by adding it to 2 tablespoons (30 ml) of cold water and setting aside. Meanwhile, in a heatproof clean glass or metal mixing bowl, use a hand mixer on medium speed to whip the egg whites to soft peaks.

Next, in a saucepan, combine the superfine sugar, corn syrup and 3 tablespoons plus 1 teaspoon (50 ml) of water, and heat over medium heat until the temperature of the mixture reaches 240°F (115°C) With the mixer on medium speed, slowly add the sugar syrup to the egg whites and whip for 2 minutes.

Then, heat the bloomed gelatin in a saucepan until it is completely melted and pour it slowly into the egg whites. Finally, add the vanilla and keep mixing for 6 to 10 minutes, or until the consistency looks like that of meringue.

DO I REALLY NEED A DIGITAL SCALE AND THERMOMETER?

I would not suggest making marshmallows without these tools. They are crucial and contribute to how your marshmallows will turn out. Without them, your marshmallows might not set or will become very hard.

WHAT CAN I USE TO DRAW THE FINAL DETAILS ONTO MY MARSHMALLOWS?

In my marshmallow recipes, I use black-colored marshmallow mixture to draw on the final details. Using this mixture will prevent the details from fading quickly once they are put in liquid. However, as it sets very fast, it is quite difficult to use, especially when you are new to making marshmallows.

Easier alternatives you could use are edible markers or edible paint. Once you are done making the marshmallows, let them air-dry for 10 to 15 minutes, then draw on the details before covering in cornstarch. However, keep in mind if they are placed in hot liquid, the details will fade much faster as opposed to when using a black marshmallow mixture to draw the details.

HOW DO I STORE MY MARSHMALLOWS?

Store your marshmallows for up to 10 days in an airtight container with a little extra cornstarch at room temperature. Never in the fridge or freezer, or else they will turn hard!

DINOSAURS IN LOVE

Difficulty level: Intermediate
Yield: 20 to 22 marshmallows

These dinosaurs are not the scary ones you may be used to—in fact, they're rather adorable! You can make single ones, but you could also make a cute couple by making two dinosaurs right next to each other. These would be great for special occasions, such as Valentine's Day or anniversaries, and you could also experiment by using different colors for the dinosaurs.

Make sure you have the following ready:

INGREDIENTS AND TOOLS

Black, red and blue gel food coloring

5 piping bags

Baking sheet

Parchment paper

Cornstarch

Dough scraper

Baking scriber or toothpicks

Small soft paintbrush

Begin by making the Basic Marshmallow Recipe on page 128. Remember not to use piping tips when making marshmallows!

PREP THE COLORS

BLACK: Take 1 tablespoon (15 ml) of the marshmallow mixture and add 4 to 5 drops of black gel food coloring. Mix in the color, using a spoon, and transfer to a piping bag.

RED: Take 1 tablespoon (15 ml) of the marshmallow mixture and add 3 to 4 drops of red gel food coloring. Mix in the color, using a spoon, and transfer to a piping bag.

DARK BLUE: Take 1 tablespoon (15 ml) of the marshmallow mixture and add 4 to 5 drops of blue gel food coloring. Mix in the color, using a spoon, and transfer to a piping bag.

WHITE: Transfer 1 teaspoon of the marshmallow mixture to a small, microwave-safe bowl and set aside (do not place in a piping bag). (No food coloring required.)

LIGHT BLUE: Take the remaining marshmallow mixture and add 2 to 3 drops of blue gel food coloring. Mix in the color, using a spatula, and transfer one-quarter to a piping bag (No. 1) and the remaining three-quarters to another piping bag (No. 2).

PIPE THE DESIGN

At some point, you will notice the marshmallow mixture has set. When this occurs, you'll need to soften it. To do this, just heat it in a microwave for 2- to 3-second intervals (it is important that you do not heat it in longer intervals). Between intervals, make sure to mix with a spatula or use your hands to massage the mixture in the piping bags until it is soft. Be careful not to overheat it!

I. Line a baking sheet with parchment paper, cutting away the excess. Cover the paper with a layer of cornstarch to $^3/_8$-inch (1-cm) depth. Use a dough scraper to even out the cornstarch, so you have an even surface to work on.

(continued)

DINOSAURS IN LOVE (CONTINUED)

2. Cut a ½-inch (1.3-cm) opening at the tip of piping bag No. 2 of the light blue marshmallow mixture. Directly onto the cornstarch, pipe the body of a dinosaur about 1 inch (2.5 cm) high and wide. Repeat to make five dinosaurs at a time.

3. Using the same piping bag, pipe the mixture onto each body and slowly drag it outward to create the tail. Use a baking scriber to blend both parts together.

4. Make a tiny cut at the tip of the piping bag of the red marshmallow mixture and pipe a small heart onto the chest of each dinosaur. Use a baking scriber to adjust the shape.

5. Make a tiny cut at the tip of the piping bag of the dark blue marshmallow mixture and pipe on the spikes of each dinosaur, starting at the top of the head and going down the tail.

6. Cut a scant ¼-inch (6-mm) opening at the tip of piping bag No. 1 of the light blue marshmallow mixture. Pipe two arms slightly over the heart and two dots to make the feet.

7. Make a tiny cut at the tip of the piping bag of the black marshmallow mixture and pipe on the eyes.

8. Dip your baking scriber into the black marshmallow mixture to draw on a smile between the eyes. This way you will create much thinner lines.

9. Lastly, use a baking scriber to take some of the white marshmallow mixture and add small dots onto the eyes.

10. Continue until you have made 20 dinosaurs in total. Or, to make cute dinosaur marshmallow couples holding hands, follow the exact same steps, piping them right next to each other before covering with cornstarch.

11. Once you are done making all your dinosaur marshmallows, carefully cover them with the remaining cornstarch, using a spoon and a clean, soft paintbrush to pat it in. Make sure they are fully covered and let them sit for 10 minutes.

12. After 10 minutes, carefully brush off the excess cornstarch, using your paintbrush. Then, transfer the marshmallows to a plate. Let them air-dry for about 2 hours before storing in an airtight container.

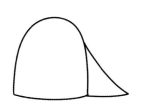

CAT PAW MARSHMALLOWS

Difficulty level: Beginner
Yield: 22 to 26 marshmallows

INGREDIENTS AND TOOLS

Pink gel food coloring

2 piping bags

Baking sheet

Parchment paper

Cornstarch

Dough scraper

Baking scriber or toothpicks

Small soft paintbrush

These cat paw marshmallows are a great design for beginners as they don't include much detail, yet they are still super adorable! For this design, we will be using white and pink, but you can choose whatever colors you want to work with, to add your own personal touch to this design.

Make sure you have the following ready:

Begin by making the Basic Marshmallow Recipe on page 128. Remember not to use piping tips when making marshmallows!

PREP THE COLORS

PINK: Place one-third of the marshmallow mixture in a mixing bowl and add 2 to 3 drops of pink gel food coloring. Use a spatula to mix in the color, then transfer to a piping bag.

WHITE: Transfer the remaining two-thirds of the marshmallow mixture directly to a piping bag. (No food coloring required.)

PIPE THE DESIGN

At some point, you will notice the marshmallow mixture has set. When this occurs, you'll need to soften it. To do this, just heat it in a microwave for 2- to 3-second intervals (it is important that you do not heat it in longer intervals). Between intervals, make sure to mix with a spatula or use your hands to massage the mixture in the piping bags until it is soft. Be careful not to overheat it!

(continued)

CAT PAW MARSHMALLOWS (CONTINUED)

1. Line a baking sheet with parchment paper, cutting away the excess. Cover with a thin layer of cornstarch to a scant ¼-inch (6-mm) depth. Use a dough scraper to even out the cornstarch, so you have an even surface to work on.

2. Make one marshmallow at a time. Cut a ½-inch (1.3-cm) opening at the tip of the piping bag of the white marshmallow mixture. Pipe directly onto the cornstarch to create the round base of the paw, about 1½ inches (4 cm) in diameter.

3. Make a scant ¼-inch (6-mm) cut at the tip of the piping bag of the pink marshmallow mixture and pipe the paw pad.

4. Then, above the paw pad, pipe four small dots to create the toes.

5. Repeat steps 2 through 4 until you have made all 24 of your marshmallow paws. If all 24 marshmallows don't fit onto your tray, make them in batches of 12 marshmallows at a time. Then, carefully cover the paws on all sides with the remaining cornstarch, using a clean, soft paintbrush to pat it in. Let them sit for 10 minutes.

6. After 10 minutes, carefully brush off the excess cornstarch, using your paintbrush, and let the marshmallows air-dry for 2 hours before storing in an airtight container.

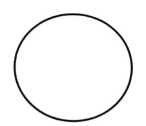

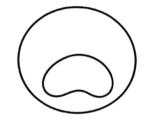

JOYFUL SEA TURTLES

Difficulty level: Intermediate
Yield: 22 to 24 marshmallows

INGREDIENTS AND TOOLS

Black, green and brown gel food coloring

4 piping bags

Baking sheet

Parchment paper

Cornstarch

Dough scraper

Baking scriber or toothpicks

Small soft paintbrush

Sea turtles are one of my favorite animals. I had made sea turtle meringue cookies before, but never as marshmallows prior to now. To be honest, I think they are even more fun as marshmallows because of how squishy they are! To make these more beginner-friendly, replace the black marshmallow mixture with black edible paint to draw the final details of the sea turtles.

Make sure you have the following ready:

Begin by making the Basic Marshmallow Recipe on page 128. Remember not to use piping tips when making marshmallows!

PREP THE COLORS

BLACK: Take 1 tablespoon (15 ml) of the marshmallow mixture and add 3 to 4 drops of black gel food coloring. Mix in the color with a spoon and transfer to a piping bag.

WHITE: Transfer 1 teaspoon of the marshmallow mixture to a piping bag. You will only need a very small amount.

Divide the remaining marshmallow mixture equally between two separate mixing bowls, to make the following colors.

GREEN: To the first portion, add 3 to 5 drops of green gel food coloring. Mix in the color, using a spatula, and transfer to a piping bag.

BROWN: To the second portion, add 3 to 4 drops of brown gel food coloring and mix in the color, using a spatula. Transfer one-quarter of this portion to a piping bag (No. 1) and the other three-quarters of this portion to another piping bag (No. 2).

PIPE THE DESIGN

At some point, you will notice the marshmallow mixture has set. When this occurs, you'll need to soften it. To do this, just heat it in a microwave for 2- to 3-second intervals (it is important that you do not heat it in longer intervals). Between intervals, make sure to mix with a spatula or use your hands to massage the mixture in the piping bags until it is soft. Be careful not to overheat it!

(continued)

JOYFUL SEA TURTLES
(CONTINUED)

1. Line a baking sheet with parchment paper and cut away the excess. Cover the parchment paper with a thin layer of cornstarch to a ³/₈-inch (1-cm) depth. Use a dough scraper to even out the cornstarch, so you have an even surface to work on.

2. Cut a ½-inch (1.3-cm) opening at the tip of piping bag No. 2 of the brown marshmallow mixture. Directly onto the cornstarch, pipe a ball shape about 1¼ inches (3 cm) in diameter. Repeat to pipe five turtle marshmallows at a time.

3. Make a small cut at the tip of piping bag No. 1 of the brown marshmallow mixture. Use it to pipe a rim around the edges of each of the balls you just made.

4. Then, cut a scant ¼-inch (6-mm) opening at the tip of the piping bag of the green marshmallow mixture. Use it to pipe the head, arms, legs and tail of each turtle.

5. Make a small cut at the tip of the piping bag of the black marshmallow mixture, just enough to pipe on the eyes, and pipe a small amount onto a plate.

6. Use a baking scriber to dip this into the black marshmallow mixture and carefully draw the shell pattern onto the sea turtles.

7. Use the same method to draw on the eyebrows and a cute smile to finish them off.

8. After you are done making all 22 sea turtles, carefully cover your marshmallows on all sides with the remaining cornstarch, using a spoon and a clean, soft paintbrush to pat it in. Make sure they are fully covered and let them sit for 10 minutes. If you can't fit all 22 sea turtles onto your tray, make them in batches of 11 marshmallows at a time.

9. After 10 minutes, carefully brush off the excess cornstarch, using your paintbrush, and transfer the marshmallows to a plate. Let them air-dry for about 2 hours before storing them in an airtight container.

CUTEST CORGI BUTTS

Difficulty level: Intermediate
Yield: 24 to 26 marshmallows

These squishy corgi butts were the first marshmallows I ever made. Still to this day, I think these are one of my favorites!

The trickiest part of these marshmallows is to make the small details, such as the paws and tail, stand out. If your marshmallow mixture is too soft, the paws and tail of the corgi will just blend in together with the rest. If this is the case, let the mixture sit for few minutes until it becomes thicker again. I recommend testing it first to check the consistency before piping the paws and tail onto the marshmallows. Once you pipe them onto the marshmallows, it will be very difficult to correct them.

Make sure you have the following ready:

INGREDIENTS AND TOOLS

Pink (or light beige), brown and orange gel food coloring

4 piping bags

Baking sheet

Parchment paper

Cornstarch

Dough scraper

Baking scriber or toothpicks

Small soft paintbrush

Cornstarch

Begin by making the Basic Marshmallow Recipe on page 128. Remember not to use piping tips when making marshmallows!

PREP THE COLORS

LIGHT PINK: Take 1 tablespoon (15 g) of the marshmallow mixture and add 1 drop of pink gel food coloring to create a very light pink color. Alternatively, use 2 drops of light beige gel food coloring. Mix in the color, using a small spoon, then transfer to a piping bag and set aside.

Divide the remaining marshmallow mixture equally between two separate mixing bowls, to make the following colors.

ORANGE-BROWN: To one portion, add 2 drops of brown gel food coloring and 3 to 4 drops of orange gel food coloring. Mix in the color, using a spatula, then transfer to a piping bag.

WHITE: Divide the second portion between two piping bags: one-third into one piping bag (No. 1) and the other two-thirds into a different piping bag (No. 2). This part does not require any food coloring as it remains white.

PIPE THE DESIGN

At some point, you will notice the marshmallow mixture has set. When this occurs, you'll need to soften it. To do this, just heat it in a microwave for 2- to 3-second intervals (it is important that you do not heat it in longer intervals). Between intervals, make sure to mix with a spatula or use your hands to massage the mixture in the piping bags until it is soft. Be careful not to overheat it!

(continued)

CUTEST CORGI BUTTS
(CONTINUED)

1. Line a baking sheet with parchment paper, cutting away any excess. Cover with a thin layer of cornstarch to a scant ¼-inch (6-mm) depth. Use a dough scraper to even out the cornstarch, so you have an even surface to work on. For this recipe, you should make only two corgi butts at a time so the orange-brown (the upper part) and white marshmallow mixture (for the butt cheeks) can blend in together while the marshmallow mixtures are soft.

2. Cut a scant ¼-inch (6-mm) opening at the tip of the piping bag of the orange-brown marshmallow mixture. Pipe the upper part of each corgi butt directly onto the cornstarch, about 1½ inches (4 cm) in width and ½ inch (1.3 cm) in height.

3. Cut a ½-inch (1.3-cm) opening at the tip of piping bag No. 2 of the white marshmallow mixture. Use this to pipe the butt cheeks. Use a baking scriber to blend both the white and orange-brown parts together. The corgi butts should be about 1½ inches (4 cm) in height and in width.

4. Then, cut a scant ¼-inch (6-mm) opening at the tip of piping bag No. 1 of the white marshmallow mixture and pipe on the feet.

5. Use the orange-brown marshmallow mixture to pipe a tail onto each butt.

6. Lastly, make a tiny cut at the tip of the piping bag of light pink marshmallow mixture to pipe on the paw pads onto the feet. There you have it! Two cute tiny corgi butts. Repeat until you have made all 24 of your marshmallows. If you can't fit all 24 marshmallows onto your tray, make them in batches of 8 or 12 at a time.

7. Once you are done making the corgi butt marshmallows, carefully cover on all sides with the remaining cornstarch, using a spoon and a clean, soft paintbrush to pat it in. Make sure they're fully covered and let them sit for 10 minutes.

8. After 10 minutes, brush off the excess cornstarch, using your paintbrush, and transfer the marshmallows to a plate to air-dry for about 2 hours before storing them in an airtight container.

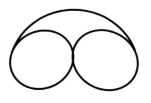

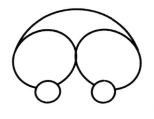

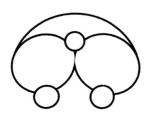

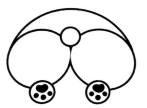

FUN YELLOW DUCKS

Difficulty level: Intermediate
Yield: 24 to 26 marshmallows

INGREDIENTS AND TOOLS

Black, orange and yellow gel food coloring

5 piping bags

Baking sheet

Parchment paper

Cornstarch

Dough scraper

Baking scriber or toothpicks

Small soft paintbrush

These yellow duck marshmallows are squishy and look just like miniature rubber duck toys! These are great to make for birthday parties, like when I made them for my nephew's first birthday. You can give them away as gifts, decorate cakes with them or surprise your guests by adding a cute little duck marshmallow in their drink.

Make sure you have the following ready:

Begin by making the Basic Marshmallow Recipe on page 128. Remember not to use piping tips when making marshmallows!

PREP THE COLORS

WHITE: Take 1 tablespoon (15 ml) of the marshmallow mixture and transfer it directly to a piping bag. (No food coloring required.)

BLACK: Transfer another tablespoon (15 ml) of the marsh-mallow mixture and add 3 to 5 drops of black gel food coloring. Mix in the color, using a spoon, and transfer to a piping bag.

ORANGE: Transfer one-quarter of the remaining marshmallow mixture to a mixing bowl and add 3 to 4 drops of orange gel food coloring. Mix in the color, using a spatula, and transfer to a piping bag.

YELLOW: To the remaining three-quarters of the marshmallow mixture, add 5 to 6 drops of yellow gel food coloring. Use a spatula to mix in the color, then transfer one-third to a piping bag (No. 1) and two-thirds to another piping bag (No. 2).

PIPE THE DESIGN

At some point, you will notice the marshmallow mixture has set. When this occurs, you'll need to soften it. To do this, just heat it in a microwave for 2- to 3-second intervals (it is important that you do not heat it in longer intervals). Between intervals, make sure to mix with a spatula or use your hands to massage the mixture in the piping bags until it is soft. Be careful not to overheat it!

(continued)

FUN YELLOW DUCKS (CONTINUED)

1. Line a baking sheet with parchment and cut away any excess. Cover with a thin layer of cornstarch, a scant ¼-inch (6-mm) depth. Use a dough scraper to even out the cornstarch, so you have an even surface to work on.

2. Cut a ½-inch (1.3-cm) opening at the tip of piping bag No. 2 of the yellow marshmallow mixture. Directly onto the cornstarch, first pipe the body of a duck, about 1½ inches (4 cm) in diameter. The technique used here is to squeeze, slowly release and drag away toward the end to create the tail of the duck. Repeat this step to create 24 duck bodies. If all 24 don't fit onto your tray, make the ducks in batches of 12 marshmallows at a time, leaving about 3 inches (7.5 cm) between the marshmallows.

3. Use the same piping bag with yellow marshmallow to pipe the head, about ¾ inch (2 cm) in diameter. Use a baking scriber or toothpick to adjust the shape a little, if needed. Repeat until each duck body has a head.

4. Cut a scant ¼-inch (6-mm) opening at the tip of piping bag No. 1 of the yellow marshmallow mixture. Use it to pipe on the wing of the duck in small strokes.

5. Cut a scant ¼-inch (6-mm) opening at the tip of the piping bag of the orange marshmallow mixture. Pipe a beak onto each duck.

6. Make a tiny cut at the tip of the piping bag of the black marshmallow and use it to pipe one small dot onto the head to create an eye.

7. Dip your baking scriber into the black meringue and draw one dot onto the beak.

8. Lastly, make a tiny cut at the tip of the white marshmallow mixture. Pipe a small amount onto your baking scriber and add one small dot onto the eye to create that cute glossy effect.

9. Once you're done making all the duck marshmallows, cover on all sides with the remaining cornstarch, using a spoon or clean, soft paintbrush to pat it in. Make sure they are fully covered and let them sit for 10 minutes.

10. Carefully brush off the excess cornstarch, using your paintbrush, and transfer the marshmallows to a plate. Let them air-dry for about 2 hours before storing them in an airtight container.

BEAUTIFUL BLOOMING FLOWERS

Difficulty level: Advanced
Yield: 14 to 16 marshmallows

What makes these flowers so special, is that they bloom once you put them in hot chocolate, coffee or any other hot beverage. Your guests will be so surprised when they see the marshmallows bloom and will think you have put in a lot of effort into making them!

Make sure you have the following ready:

INGREDIENTS AND TOOLS

Yellow and pink gel food coloring

3 piping bags

Baking sheet

Parchment paper

Cornstarch

Dough scraper

Baking scriber or toothpicks

Small soft paintbrush

Green chocolate melts

Silicone mini muffin or ice cube mold

Begin by making the Basic Marshmallow Recipe on page 128. Remember not to use piping tips when making marshmallows!

PREP THE COLORS

YELLOW: Take 1 tablespoon (15 ml) of the marshmallow mixture and add 2 drops of yellow gel food coloring. Mix in the color, using a spoon, and transfer to a piping bag.

WHITE: Transfer one-third of the remaining marshmallow mixture directly to a piping bag. (No food coloring required.)

BRIGHT PINK: To the remaining two-thirds of the marshmallow mixture, add 4 to 6 drops of pink gel food coloring. Mix in the color, using a spatula, and transfer to a piping bag.

PIPE THE DESIGN

At some point, you will notice the marshmallow mixture has set. When this occurs, you'll need to soften it. To do this, just heat it in a microwave for 2- to 3-second intervals (it is important that you do not heat it in longer intervals). Between intervals, make sure to mix with a spatula or use your hands to massage the mixture in the piping bags until it is soft. Be careful not to overheat it!

I. Line a baking sheet with parchment paper and cut away any excess. Cover with a thin layer of cornstarch to a scant ¼-inch (6-mm) depth. Use a dough scraper to even out the cornstarch, so you have an even surface to work on.

(continued)

BEAUTIFUL BLOOMING FLOWERS (CONTINUED)

PINK FLOWER

2. To create a pink flower, cut a scant ¼-inch (6-mm) opening at the tip of the piping bag of the pink marshmallow mixture. Pipe a first layer of flower petals and let them sit for 5 minutes. Each flower should be about 3½ inches (9 cm).

3. Then, use the same pink marshmallow mixture to pipe another layer of flower petals (slightly smaller) than the first layer we made. Let it sit for 5 minutes.

4. Lastly, make a tiny cut at the tip of the piping bag of your yellow marshmallow mixture and pipe little dots in the middle of the pink flower. Your pink flower is now done!

DAISY

5. To create a daisy flower, cut a scant ¼-inch (6-mm) opening at the tip of the piping bag of your white marshmallow mixture and pipe 8 flower petals. These flowers should also be about 3½ inches (9 cm) each.

6. Use the yellow marshmallow mixture to pipe one dot in the middle of the flower.

7. Once you are done making all your flower marshmallows, carefully cover them with the remaining cornstarch, using a spoon or clean, soft paintbrush, making sure they are fully covered. Let them sit in the cornstarch for 10 minutes.

8. Carefully brush off the excess cornstarch, using your paintbrush, then transfer the marshmallows to a plate. Let them air-dry for about 2 hours.

9. Melt some green chocolate melts (see page 180 for how to do this). Cover the insides of your silicone mini muffin or ice cube mold with the melted chocolate, using a small teaspoon or clean paintbrush to coat the sides.

10. Take one of your flower marshmallows and fold the outer ends together so it fits into a section of the mold. Repeat to fit the flowers into the other molds. Transfer the baking sheet of marshmallows to the fridge to chill for 10 to 15 minutes, then carefully remove them from the molds.

Now you can just put them in hot chocolate and see the magic happen in front of you!

SWEET DOH! NUTS
WITH SPRINKLES

Difficulty level: Beginner
Yield: 22 to 24 marshmallows

INGREDIENTS AND TOOLS

Pink, brown, blue, red and yellow gel food coloring

5 piping bags

Baking sheet

Parchment paper

Cornstarch

Dough scraper

Baking scriber or toothpicks

Small soft paintbrush

These donut marshmallows were inspired by the iconic Homer Simpson donuts, but you can be creative as you like! Use different colors for the "glaze," or even use real sprinkles to decorate them. It is also fun to use different extracts in place of the usual vanilla extract to flavor your marshmallows. I used strawberry extract for my donut marshmallows because of the pink glaze, but you could also use banana, cinnamon or orange extract, as a few examples.

Make sure you have the following ready:

Begin by making the Basic Marshmallow Recipe on page 128. Remember not to use piping tips when making marshmallows!

PREP THE COLORS

PINK: Place one-quarter of the marshmallow mixture in a mixing bowl and add 4 to 5 drops of pink gel food coloring. You want a bright pink color for the glaze, so add an additional 2 to 3 drops of pink gel food coloring if you are not satisfied yet with the color. Mix the food coloring with a spatula, transfer to a piping bag and set aside.

BROWN: Transfer one-half of the remaining marshmallow mixture to a separate mixing bowl and add 2 to 3 drops of brown gel food coloring and 1 drop of yellow gel food coloring. Add an additional 1 to 2 drops of brown or yellow food coloring until you are satisfied with the color. Use a spatula to mix in the color, then transfer to a piping bag.

Divide the remaining one-quarter of the marshmallow mixture equally among three separate small mixing bowls to make the following colors. These will be our donut sprinkles.

BLUE: To the first portion, add 2 drops of blue gel food coloring. Mix in the color with a spoon and transfer to a piping bag.

RED: To the second portion, add 2 to 3 drops of red gel food coloring. Mix in the color with a spoon and transfer to a piping bag.

YELLOW: To the third portion, add 2 drops of yellow gel food coloring. Mix in the color with a spoon and transfer to a piping bag.

(continued)

SWEET DOH! NUTS WITH SPRINKLES (CONTINUED)

PIPE THE DESIGN

At some point, you will notice the marshmallow mixture has set. When this occurs, you'll need to soften it. To do this, just heat it in a microwave for 2- to 3-second intervals (it is important that you do not heat it in longer intervals). Between intervals, make sure to mix with a spatula or use your hands to massage the mixture in the piping bags until it is soft. Be careful not to overheat it!

1. Line a baking sheet with parchment paper and cut away any excess. Cover with a thin layer of cornstarch to a scant ¼-inch (0.6-mm) depth. Use a dough scraper to even out the cornstarch, so you have an even surface to work on.

2. Cut a ½-inch (1.3-cm) opening at the tip of the piping bag with the brown marshmallow mixture.

3. Use the brown marshmallow mixture to pipe 1½- to 2-inch (4- to 5-cm)-diameter circles to form the donuts, leaving the center hollow (see image). Make 8 to 10 donuts at a time.

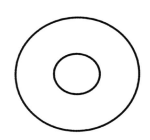

4. Make a small cut at the tip of the piping bag with the pink marshmallow mixture. Pipe the "glaze" in a zigzag motion on top of the donuts. Use a baking scriber to adjust the shape, if needed, but do this quickly before they set!

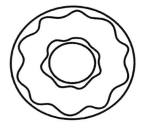

5. Lastly, make a tiny cut at the tip of the respective piping bags of your blue, yellow and red marshmallow mixtures—just enough to get the mixture out. Pipe random small stripes onto the pink glaze to make the sprinkles on the donuts.

6. Once you're done making all the donuts, cover on all sides with the remaining cornstarch, using a spoon and clean, soft paintbrush to pat it in. Make sure they are fully covered and let them sit for 10 minutes.

7. Carefully brush off the excess cornstarch, using your paintbrush, and transfer the marshmallows to a plate. Let them air-dry for about 2 hours before storing them in an airtight container.

HAPPY CLOUDS

Difficulty level: Beginner
Yield: 14 to 16 marshmallows

INGREDIENTS AND TOOLS

Black and pink gel food coloring

3 piping bags

Baking sheet

Parchment paper

Cornstarch

Dough scraper

Baking scriber or toothpicks

Small soft paintbrush

These marshmallows are great for beginners! They are very easy to make and yet very versatile. In this recipe, I will show you examples of different facial expressions that you could give them.

If you find it difficult to make the small facial features using the marshmallow mixture, you could also use edible paint to draw them on. Just keep in mind that edible paint fades a lot faster in liquid. So, if you want to make hot cocoa bombs with these marshmallows, I recommend making the facial features using the marshmallow mixture. You could also pair these cloud marshmallows with other fun marshmallows, such as the Sleepy Bears (page 157).

Make sure you have the following ready:

Begin by making the Basic Marshmallow Recipe on page 128. Remember not to use piping tips when making marshmallows!

PREP THE COLORS

BLACK: Take 1 tablespoon (15 ml) of the marshmallow mixture and add 4 to 5 drops of black gel food coloring. Mix in the color, using a spoon, and transfer to a piping bag.

LIGHT PINK: Take 1 tablespoon (15 ml) of the marshmallow mixture and add 1 drop of pink gel food coloring. Mix in the color, using a spoon, and transfer to a piping bag.

WHITE: Transfer the remaining marshmallow mixture directly to a piping bag. (No food coloring required.)

PIPE THE DESIGN

At some point, you will notice the marshmallow mixture has set. When this occurs, you'll need to soften it. To do this, just heat it in a microwave for 2- to 3-second intervals (it is important that you do not heat it in longer intervals). Between intervals, make sure to mix with a spatula or use your hands to massage the mixture in the piping bags until it is soft. Be careful not to overheat it!

1. Line a baking sheet with parchment paper, cutting away any excess. Cover with a thin layer of cornstarch to a scant ¼-inch (6-mm) depth. Use a dough scraper to even out the cornstarch, so you have an even surface to work on.

(continued)

HAPPY CLOUDS (CONTINUED)

2. Cut a ½-inch (1.3-cm) opening at the tip of the piping bag of the white marshmallow mixture. Directly onto the cornstarch, pipe small dots (connected to one another) to make the clouds. Use a baking scriber or toothpick to soften any edges. They should each be around 1½ to 2 inches (4 to 5 cm) across. Repeat this step until you almost have a full baking sheet of little cloud marshmallows.

3. Then, make a small cut at the tip of the piping bag of your black marshmallow mixture, just enough to get the marshmallow mixture out to pipe on the eyes.

4. Dip your baking scriber into the black marshmallow mixture to draw on the mouth. I added a few fun facial expression examples you could make.

5. You could leave the eyes as they are, or if you want to give them a glossy look, use your baking scriber to take some of the white marshmallow mixture and add tiny dots to the eyes.

6. Make a tiny cut at the tip of the piping bag of your light pink marshmallow mixture and pipe on the blushing cheeks. Let the clouds sit for 10 minutes.

7. Carefully cover on all sides with the remaining cornstarch, using a spoon and a clean, soft paintbrush to pat it in. Make sure they are fully covered and let them sit for another 10 minutes.

8. Pick them up one by one and carefully brush off the excess cornstarch. Transfer the marshmallows to a plate and let them air-dry for about 2 hours before storing them in an airtight container.

SLEEPY BEARS ON HAPPY CLOUDS

Difficulty level: Intermediate
Yield: 20 to 22 marshmallows

The fun part about marshmallows is that you can also pair them. I paired these sleepy bears with my Happy Clouds marshmallows (page 153) so it looks as if they are sleeping on clouds. You could leave them as two separate marshmallows or add a small dot of melted chocolate to make the two marshmallows stick together.

Make sure you have the following ready:

Begin by making the Basic Marshmallow Recipe on page 128. Remember not to use piping tips when making marshmallows!

PREP THE COLORS

BLACK: Take 1 tablespoon (15 ml) of the marshmallow mixture and add 4 to 5 drops of black gel food coloring. Mix in the color, using a spoon, and transfer to a piping bag.

LIGHT PINK: Take 1 tablespoon (15 ml) of the marshmallow mixture and add 1 drop of pink gel food coloring. Mix in the color, using a spoon, and transfer to a piping bag.

LIGHT BROWN: Place one-quarter of the remaining marsh-mallow mixture in a mixing bowl and add 1 drop of brown gel food coloring. Mix in the color, using a spatula, and transfer to a piping bag.

BROWN: To the remaining three-quarters of the marshmallow mixture, add 3 to 5 drops of brown gel food coloring and 1 drop of yellow gel food coloring. You could leave out the yellow, but it adds some warmth to the color. Mix in the coloring, using a spatula, and transfer one-third to a piping bag (No. 1), and two-thirds to another piping bag (No. 2).

INGREDIENTS AND TOOLS

Black, pink, brown and yellow gel food coloring

5 piping bags

Baking sheet

Parchment paper

Cornstarch

Dough scraper

Baking scriber or toothpicks

Small soft paintbrush

PIPE THE DESIGN

At some point, you will notice the marshmallow mixture has set. When this occurs, you'll need to soften it. To do this, just heat it in a microwave for 2- to 3-second intervals (it is important that you do not heat it in longer intervals). Between intervals, make sure to mix with a spatula or use your hands to massage the mixture in the piping bags until it is soft. Be careful not to overheat it!

1. Line a baking sheet, cutting away any excess. Cover the parchment paper with a layer of cornstarch to a $^3/_8$-inch (1-cm) depth. Use a dough scraper to even out the cornstarch, so you have an even surface to work on.

(continued)

SLEEPY BEARS ON HAPPY CLOUDS (CONTINUED)

2. Cut a ½-inch (1.3-cm) opening at the tip of piping bag No. 2 of the brown marshmallow mixture.

3. Pipe a 1-inch (2.5-cm) round shape to make the body of the bear and a slightly smaller round shape to make its head. Make five bear marshmallows at a time.

4. Cut a scant ¼-inch (6-mm) opening at the tip of piping bag No. 1 of the brown marshmallow mixture. Use it to pipe the ears, arms, legs and tail. Use a baking scriber to soften the edges.

5. Use the light brown marshmallow mixture to pipe the snout and inside of the ears.

6. Make a tiny cut at the tip of the piping bag of the black marshmallow mixture and pipe on the nose. Dip your baking scriber into the black color of the nose and draw two C-shaped lines to make the mouth of the bear. Then, using the same method, draw on the eyes.

7. Lastly, make a tiny cut at the tip of the piping bag of the light pink marshmallow mixture and pipe two small dots onto the face.

8. Once you are done making all your marshmallows, carefully cover them on all sides with the remaining cornstarch, using a spoon and a clean, soft paintbrush to pat it in. Make sure they are fully covered and let them sit for 10 minutes.

9. After 10 minutes, carefully brush off the excess cornstarch, using a clean, soft paintbrush, and transfer the marshmallows to a plate. Let them air-dry for about 2 hours before storing in an airtight container.

10. Match your cute sleepy bear marshmallows together with the happy clouds. Simply place them on top of each other or use a small dot of melted chocolate to make them stick.

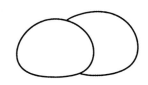

3

4

5

6

7

RELAXING PIGS

Difficulty level: Intermediate
Yield: 20 to 22 marshmallows

INGREDIENTS AND TOOLS

Black and pink gel food coloring

3 piping bags

Baking sheet

Parchment paper

Cornstarch

Dough scraper

Baking scriber or toothpicks

Small soft paintbrush

These relaxing pigs are inspired by my lazy cat marshmallows that I posted on my social media. Not only are they fun to make, but they are also fun to play with, especially their big bellies!

Imagine making a farm-themed cake topped with chocolate ganache or melted chocolate and these cute little marshmallow pigs on top. It would just look as though they are having a great time lying in the mud.

Make sure you have the following ready:

Begin by making the Basic Marshmallow Recipe on page 128. Remember not to use piping tips when making marshmallows!

PREP THE COLORS

BLACK: Take 1 tablespoon (15 ml) of the marshmallow mixture and add 2 to 3 drops of black gel food coloring. Mix in the coloring, using a small spoon or spatula, and transfer to a piping bag.

PINK: To the remaining marshmallow mixture, add 3 to 4 drops of pink gel food coloring. Mix in the coloring, using a spatula. Transfer one-third of the pink marshmallow mixture to a piping bag (No. 1), and two-thirds of the pink marshmallow mixture to another piping bag (No. 2).

PIPE THE DESIGN

At some point, you will notice the marshmallow mixture has set. When this occurs, you'll need to soften it. To do this, just heat it in a microwave for 2- to 3-second intervals (it is important that you do not heat it in longer intervals). Between intervals, make sure to mix with a spatula or use your hands to massage the mixture in the piping bags until it is soft. Be careful not to overheat it!

1. Line a baking sheet with parchment paper, cutting away any excess. Cover with a thin layer of cornstarch to a scant ¼-inch (6-mm) depth. Use a dough scraper to even out the cornstarch, so you have an even surface to work on.

(continued)

RELAXING PIGS
(CONTINUED)

2. Make three marshmallows at a time. Cut a ½-inch (1.3-cm) opening at the tip of piping bag No. 2 of the pink marshmallow mixture. Directly onto the cornstarch, pipe the belly of the pigs first, about 1 inch (2.5 cm) in diameter.

3. Then, make a small cut at the tip of piping bag No. 1 of the pink marshmallow mixture and pipe the arms and legs.

4. Switch back to using the other pink marshmallow mixture (piping bag No. 2) to pipe the head and make sure it slightly overlaps the arms.

5. Then switch to piping bag No. 1 of the pink marshmallow mixture once more to pipe the snout and ears of the pigs. Adjust the shape or edges, using a baking scriber or toothpick. Be sure to do this immediately before they set!

6. To make the final black details, use the black marshmallow mixture to pipe a small amount onto a plate and dip your baking scriber into it to draw on the eyes, nostrils and belly button.

7. Repeat steps 2 through 6 until you have made all of your marshmallows. If all 20 to 22 pigs don't fit onto your tray, make them in batches of 10 or 12 marshmallows at a time. Once they are done, let your marshmallows sit for 10 minutes before covering them in cornstarch. Use a spoon to scoop the remaining cornstarch over the pigs and use a clean, soft paintbrush to pat it in. Really make sure the marshmallows are fully covered! Let them sit again for 10 minutes.

8. After 10 minutes, carefully brush off the excess cornstarch and transfer the marshmallows to a plate. Let them air-dry for 2 hours before storing in an airtight container.

2

3

4

5

6

SPOOKY LITTLE GHOSTS

Difficulty level: Beginner
Yield: 25 to 27 marshmallows

INGREDIENTS AND TOOLS

Black gel food coloring

3 piping bags

Baking sheet

Parchment paper

Cornstarch

Dough scraper

Baking scriber or toothpicks

Small soft paintbrush

These marshmallows are perfect for Halloween and easy to make! I once made these spooky marshmallows to decorate my macarons. All you have to do is pipe a small dot of melted white chocolate onto the macaron and stick the spooky marshmallows on top. You could also use them to decorate other treats, such as cookies, donuts or brownies. Just make sure your treats are fully cooled before adding the marshmallows; then, they are ready for any Halloween party!

Make sure you have the following ready:

Begin by making the Basic Marshmallow Recipe on page 128. Remember not to use piping tips when making marshmallows!

PREP THE COLORS

BLACK: Transfer 1 tablespoon (15 ml) of the marshmallow mixture to a small mixing bowl and add 4 to 5 drops of black gel food coloring. Mix in the color, using a spoon, and transfer to a piping bag.

WHITE: Transfer one-quarter of the remaining marshmallow mixture to a piping bag (No. 1) and the other three-quarters to another piping bag (No. 2); no food coloring needed.

PIPE THE DESIGN

At some point, you will notice the marshmallow mixture has set. When this occurs, you'll need to soften it. To do this, just heat it in a microwave for 2- to 3-second intervals (it is important that you do not heat it in longer intervals). Between intervals, make sure to mix or use your hands to massage the mixture in the piping bags until it is soft. Be careful not to overheat it!

(continued)

SPOOKY LITTLE GHOSTS (CONTINUED)

1. Line a baking sheet with parchment paper, cutting away any excess. Cover with a thin layer of cornstarch to a scant ¼-inch (6-mm) depth. Use a dough scraper to even out the cornstarch, so you have an even surface to work on.

2. Cut a ½-inch (1.3-cm) opening at the tip of piping bag No. 2 of the white marshmallow mixture. Directly onto the cornstarch, pipe a teardrop shape to create the ghost's body. Make all the ghosts' bodies at once, each about 1½ inches (4 cm) long. If you can't fit all the spooky ghosts onto your tray, make them in stages of 10 or 12 marshmallows at a time.

3. Take the piping bag with black marshmallow mixture to make a small cut, just enough to get the mixture out, then pipe two small dots for the eyes.

4. Use your baking scriber to take some of the black marshmallow mixture and draw cute little smiles on the ghosts. Pipe a small amount of white marshmallow mixture onto your baking scriber and press two small dots onto the eyes.

5. Cut a scant ¼-inch (6-mm) opening at the tip of piping bag No. 1 of the white marshmallow mixture. Use it to pipe all the arms. You can pipe the arms in different directions (see illustrations).

6. Once you are done making all the spooky ghosts, cover them on all sides with the remaining cornstarch, using a spoon and a clean, soft paintbrush to pat it in. Make sure they are fully covered and let them sit for 10 minutes.

7. Carefully brush off the excess cornstarch, using your paintbrush, and transfer the marshmallows to a plate. Let them air-dry for about 2 hours before storing them in an airtight container.

COZY GINGERBREAD MEN

Difficulty level: Intermediate
Yield: 20 to 22 marshmallows

When I think of Christmas, I immediately think of gingerbread houses and gingerbread men. I added about ½ teaspoon of ground cinnamon (or you could use cinnamon extract) to match the flavor with these cute gingerbread men marshmallows.

Make sure you have the following ready:

Begin by making the Basic Marshmallow Recipe on page 128. Remember not to use piping tips when making marshmallows!

PREP THE COLORS

GREEN: Take 1 tablespoon (15 ml) of the marshmallow mixture and add 2 drops of green gel food coloring. Mix in the color, using a spoon, and transfer to a piping bag.

BLACK: Take 1 tablespoon (15 ml) of the marshmallow mixture and add 3 to 4 drops of black gel food coloring. Mix in the color, using a spoon, and transfer to a piping bag.

RED: Take 2 tablespoons (30 ml) of the marshmallow mixture and add 3 to 4 drops of red gel food coloring. Mix the color in using a spoon and transfer to a piping bag.

WHITE: Transfer one-third of the remaining marshmallow mixture directly to a piping bag. (No food coloring required.)

BROWN: To the remaining marshmallow mixture, add 4 to 5 drops of brown gel food coloring and mix in the color, using a spatula. Transfer one-quarter to a piping bag (No. 1) and the other three-quarters to another piping bag (No. 2).

PIPE THE DESIGN

At some point, you will notice the marshmallow mixture has set. When this occurs, you'll need to soften it. To do this, just heat it in a microwave for 2- to 3-second intervals (it is important that you do not heat it in longer intervals). Between intervals, make sure to mix with a spatula or use your hands to massage the mixture in the piping bags until it is soft. Be careful not to overheat it!

I. Line a baking sheet with parchment paper, cutting away any excess. Cover the parchment paper with a layer of cornstarch to a $^3/_8$-inch (1-cm) depth. Use a dough scraper to even out the cornstarch, so you have an even surface to work on.

(continued)

COZY GINGERBREAD MEN

(CONTINUED)

2. Cut a ½-inch (1.3-cm) opening in the tip of piping bag No. 2 of the brown marshmallow mixture. Use it to pipe a ball shape about 1 inch (2.5 cm) in diameter to make the body, and then make the head about the same size. For this recipe, make only two gingerbread men at a time. This is so the texture of the piped marshmallow stays wet and workable. If you let your marshmallows sit for too long, they will slowly start to set and will be very difficult to work with afterward.

3. Cut a scant ¼-inch (6-mm) opening in the tip of piping bag No. 1 of the brown marshmallow mixture. Pipe the arms and legs of each gingerbread man and use a baking scriber to adjust the shape and edges, if needed.

4. Then, take the red marshmallow mixture and cut a scant ¼-inch (6-mm) opening in the tip of the piping bag. Pipe on the scarf of the gingerbread man. Adjust the shape a little, using your baking scriber.

5. Make a tiny cut at the tip of the piping bag of the white marshmallow mixture, just enough to get out the mixture.

Use it to pipe, in a zigzag motion, the pattern on the arms, legs and head.

6. Make a tiny cut at the tip of the piping bag of the green marshmallow mixture and pipe three small dots onto the body for the buttons.

7. Make a tiny cut at the tip of the piping bag of the black marshmallow mixture and pipe two small dots to make the eyes. Dip your baking scriber into the black marshmallow mixture and draw on a smile.

8. Take some of the white marshmallow mixture with a baking scriber and add small white dots onto the eyes to create that cute and glossy look. Repeat steps 2 through 7 until you have a full baking sheet of marshmallows.

9. Once you are done making all the marshmallows, carefully cover them on all sides with the remaining cornstarch, using a spoon and a clean, soft paintbrush to pat it in. Make sure they are fully covered and let them sit for 10 minutes. If you can't fit all 20 to 22 marshmallows onto your tray, make them in batches of 10 or 11 instead.

10. After 10 minutes, carefully brush off the excess cornstarch, using a clean, soft paintbrush and transfer the marshmallows to a plate. Let them air-dry for about 2 hours before storing in an airtight container.

CHILLY CHRISTMAS PENGUINS

Difficulty level: Advanced
Yield: 20 to 22 marshmallows

These adorable penguins are perfect for the winter season. You could also add a Christmas hat to make a holiday-inspired marshmallow. I like to add these to my hot chocolate bombs (page 180) to give my guests a cute little surprise, but you could also use any of the other Christmas-themed marshmallows (see pages 175 and 177).

Make sure you have the following ready:

Begin by making the Basic Marshmallow Recipe on page 128. Remember not to use piping tips when making marshmallows!

PREP THE COLORS

BLUE: Take 1 tablespoon (15 ml) of the marshmallow mixture and add 3 to 4 drops of blue gel food coloring. Mix in the color with a spoon and transfer to a piping bag.

ORANGE: Take 1 tablespoon (15 ml) of the marshmallow mixture and add 2 drops of orange gel food coloring. Mix in the color with a spoon and transfer to a piping bag.

RED: Take 2 tablespoons (30 ml) of the marshmallow mixture and add 4 to 5 drops of red gel food coloring. Mix in the color, using a spoon or spatula, and transfer to a piping bag.

WHITE: Transfer one-third of the remaining marshmallow mixture directly to a piping bag. (No food coloring required.)

BLACK: To the remaining two-thirds of the marshmallow mixture, add a pea-sized drop of black gel food coloring. Mix in the color, using a spatula, and transfer one-third of the black marshmallow mixture to a piping bag (No. 1), and the other two-thirds of the black marshmallow mixture to another piping bag (No. 2).

PIPE THE DESIGN

At some point, you will notice the marshmallow mixture has set. When this occurs, you'll need to soften it. To do this, just heat it in a microwave for 2- to 3-second intervals (it is important that you do not heat it in longer intervals). Between intervals, make sure to mix with a spatula or use your hands to massage the mixture in the piping bags until it is soft. Be careful not to overheat it!

I. Line a baking sheet with parchment paper, cutting away any excess. Cover with a thin layer of cornstarch to a scant ¼-inch (6-mm) depth. Use a dough scraper to even out the cornstarch, so you have an even surface to work on.

(continued)

CHILLY CHRISTMAS PENGUINS (CONTINUED)

2. Cut a ½-inch (1.3-cm) opening into piping bag No. 2 of the black marshmallow mixture. Directly onto the cornstarch, pipe an oval ball shape about 1½ inches (4 cm) in diameter to make the penguin's body. For this recipe, you should make only two penguins at a time, because we do not want the marshmallows to set yet!

3. Cut a ½-inch (1.3-cm) opening at the tip of the piping bag of your white marshmallow mixture. Pipe onto the black marshmallow the white inner part of the penguin's body. Use a baking scriber to blend it out and to create a tip on the top of its head.

4. Then, cut a scant ¼-inch (6-mm) opening at the tip of the piping bag of the red marshmallow mixture. Pipe a scarf onto the penguin and adjust the shape a little, using a baking scriber.

5. Cut a scant ¼-inch (6-mm) opening at the tip of the piping bag of your blue marshmallow mixture and pipe the earmuffs.

6. Make a tiny cut at the tip of piping bag No. 1 of the black marshmallow mixture and pipe on the eyes and arms.

7. Then, make a tiny cut at the tip of the piping bag of your yellow marshmallow mixture and pipe on the beak and feet of the penguin.

8. Finally, use your baking scriber to take some of the white marshmallow mixture and add small dots onto the eyes.

9. Once you're done making all your penguin marshmallows, carefully cover them on all sides with the remaining cornstarch, using a spoon and a clean, soft paintbrush to pat it in. Make sure they are fully covered and let them sit for 10 minutes. If you can't fit all 20 to 22 penguins onto your tray, make them in batches of 10 or 12 instead.

10. After 10 minutes, carefully brush off the excess cornstarch, using a clean, soft paintbrush and transfer the marshmallows to a plate. Let them air-dry for about 2 hours before storing them in an airtight container.

SPARKLY SNOWFLAKES

Difficulty level: Beginner
Yield: 22 to 24 marshmallows

INGREDIENTS AND TOOLS

Blue gel food coloring

2 piping bags

Baking sheet

Parchment paper

Cornstarch

Dough scraper

Baking scriber or toothpicks

2 small soft paintbrushes

Edible glitter

Want to create something not too difficult yet very festive for the holidays? These sparkly snowflake marshmallows are perfect to jazz up your hot chocolate game. These would also be perfect to add to your hot chocolate bombs (page 180). Just make sure your marshmallow mixture is not too soft and do not make them too small, or else you will not be able to make those distinct lines.

Make sure you have the following ready:

Begin by making the Basic Marshmallow Recipe on page 128. Remember not to use piping tips when making marshmallows!

PREP THE COLORS

LIGHT BLUE: Place one-half of the marshmallow mixture in a mixing bowl and add 1 to 2 drops of blue gel food coloring. Mix in the color, using a spatula, and transfer to a piping bag.

WHITE: Transfer the remaining marshmallow mixture directly to a piping bag. (No food coloring required.)

PIPE THE DESIGN

At some point, you will notice the marshmallow mixture has set. When this occurs, you'll need to soften it. To do this, just heat it in a microwave for 2- to 3-second intervals (it is important that you do not heat it in longer intervals). Between intervals, make sure to mix with a spatula or use your hands to massage the mixture in the piping bags until it is soft. Be careful not to overheat it!

(continued)

SPARKLY SNOWFLAKES (CONTINUED)

1. Line a baking sheet with parchment paper, cutting away any excess. Cover the parchment paper with a layer of cornstarch to a $3/8$-inch (1-cm) depth. Use a dough scraper to even out the cornstarch, so you have an even surface to work on.

2. Start off using either the white or light blue marshmallow mixture, making a tiny cut at the tip of the piping bag.

3. Refer to the illustrations for how to pipe the snowflake and in which order. Make each snowflake about $2^3/_8$ inches (6 cm) in diameter. Repeat to form all the marshmallows. If you can't fit all the snowflakes onto your tray, make them in batches of 6 instead.

4. Once you are done making all the snowflake marshmallows, we will now add the sparkle. Use an edible glitter spray to spray the glitter on top of your marshmallows. Alternatively, dip a soft, clean paintbrush into the edible glitter and gently tap to sprinkle the glitter.

5. Then, carefully cover your snowflake marshmallows with the remaining cornstarch on all sides, using a spoon and a clean, soft paintbrush to pat it in. Make sure they are fully covered and let them sit for 10 minutes.

6. Carefully brush off the excess cornstarch with a clean, soft paintbrush and transfer the snowflakes to a plate. Let them air-dry for about 2 hours before storing in an airtight container.

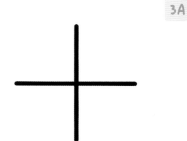
3A

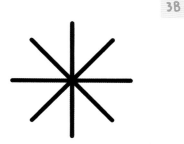
3B

3C

3D

WINTER FUN SNOWMEN

Difficulty level: Advanced
Yield: 20 to 22 marshmallows

These snowman marshmallows are a great and festive gift for special occasions during the Christmas season. You can make these snowmen two ways. In this design, we will make them 3-D, which is perfect for if you want to use them to decorate cakes, cupcakes or other treats or to just give them away as gifts. To make them more beginner-friendly, however, you can pipe them flat (2-D) and put them in hot chocolate or your hot chocolate bombs (page 180). Making them flat will really showcase these cute treats when they float in your drink.

I swapped the vanilla for mint extract to match the flavor with the design.

Make sure you have the following ready:

INGREDIENTS AND TOOLS

Brown, orange, black and red gel food coloring

6 piping bags

Baking sheet

Parchment paper

Cornstarch

Dough scraper

Baking scriber or toothpicks

Small soft paintbrush

Begin by making the Basic Marshmallow Recipe on page 128. Remember not to use piping tips when making marshmallows!

PREP THE COLORS

BROWN: Take 1 tablespoon (15 ml) of the marshmallow mixture and add 2 to 3 drops of brown gel food coloring. Mix in the color, using a spoon, and transfer to a piping bag.

ORANGE: Take 1 teaspoon of the marshmallow mixture and add 2 drops of orange gel food coloring. Mix in the color, using a spoon, and transfer to a piping bag.

BLACK: Place 2 tablespoons (30 ml) of the marshmallow mixture in a small mixing bowl and add 4 to 5 drops of black gel food coloring. Mix in the color, using a spoon, and transfer to a piping bag.

RED: Place one-quarter of the remaining marshmallow mixture in a mixing bowl and add 3 to 5 drops of red gel food coloring. Mix, using a spatula, and transfer to a piping bag.

WHITE: Transfer one-quarter of the remaining marshmallow mixture to a piping bag (No. 1), and the other remaining three-quarters to another piping bag (No. 2); no food coloring required.

PIPE THE DESIGN

At some point, you will notice the marshmallow mixture has set. When this occurs, you'll need to soften it. To do this, just heat it in a microwave for 2- to 3-second intervals (it is important that you do not heat it in longer intervals). Between intervals, make sure to mix with a spatula or use your hands to massage the mixture in the piping bags until it is soft. Be careful not to overheat it!

(continued)

WINTER FUN SNOWMEN
(CONTINUED)

1. Line a baking sheet with parchment paper, cutting away any excess. Cover the parchment paper with a layer of cornstarch $3/8$ inch (1 cm) in depth. Use a dough scraper to even out the cornstarch, so you have an even surface to work on.

2. Cut a 1/2-inch (1.3-cm) opening in the tip of piping bag No. 2 of the white marshmallow mixture. Directly onto the cornstarch, pipe a ball shape about 1 inch (2.5 cm) in diameter to make the snowman's body. Pipe five of these and let them dry for a few minutes to set slightly.

3. Next, pipe a slightly smaller ball on top of each body to create the head of the snowman. Letting the bottom part set before this step prevents the body from collapsing when you pipe on the head.

4. Make a tiny cut at the tip of the piping bag of the brown marshmallow mixture, and pipe the arms of the snowman. Start by piping the middle branch and adding two smaller branches on the side.

5. Then, cut a scant 1/4-inch (6-mm) opening in the tip of the piping bag of the red marshmallow mixture and use it to pipe on a scarf. Adjust the shape a little using a baking scriber.

6. Now, let's move on to making the hat. Cut a scant 1/4-inch (6-mm) opening at the tip of the piping bag of the black marshmallow mixture, and also at the tip of piping bag No. 1 of the white marshmallow mixture. Begin piping the rim of the hat by using black, then use white to pipe the inner rim of the hat and finish off by using black again to fill in the inner part.

7. Use the black marshmallow mixture again to pipe three small dots onto the body to make the buttons and two small dots on the face to create the eyes.

8. Use the orange marshmallow mixture to pipe on the carrot nose.

9. Lastly, dip your baking scriber into the black marshmallow mixture and draw on a cute smile.

10. Once you are done making all your snowman marshmallows, carefully cover them with the remaining cornstarch on all sides, using a spoon and a clean, soft paintbrush to pat it in. Make sure they are fully covered and let them sit for 10 minutes.

11. After 10 minutes, carefully brush off the excess cornstarch with a clean, soft paintbrush and transfer the marshmallows to a plate. Let them air-dry for about 2 hours before storing in an airtight container.

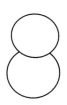

3

4

5

7A

7B

8

HOLLY JOLLY SANTA CLAUSES

Difficulty level: Advanced
Yield: 14 to 15 marshmallows

After all those Christmas-inspired marshmallows, we cannot forget about Father Christmas himself, Santa Claus! I made these marshmallows to fill my chocolate bombs, and since they are quite detailed, I piped them flat (2-D). When they burst open in hot milk, you can really showcase these beautiful marshmallows.

Make sure you have the following ready:

INGREDIENTS AND TOOLS

Black, light beige and red gel food coloring

Brown and pink gel food coloring (optional)

6 piping bags

Baking sheet

Parchment paper

Cornstarch

Dough scraper

Baking scriber or toothpicks

Small soft paintbrush

Begin by making the Basic Marshmallow Recipe on page 128. Remember not to use piping tips when making marshmallows!

PREP THE COLORS

BLACK: Take 1 tablespoon (15 ml) of the marshmallow mixture and add 4 to 5 drops of black gel food coloring. Mix in the color, using a spoon, and transfer to a piping bag.

LIGHT BEIGE: Place one-quarter of the remaining marshmallow mixture in a mixing bowl and add 3 to 4 drops of light beige gel food coloring. If you do not have light beige, add 1 drop of brown and 1 drop of pink gel good coloring;

mix to check the color and add either more brown or pink, if needed. Mix in the color with a spatula and transfer one-quarter of the light beige marshmallow mixture to a piping bag (No. 1) and the remaining three-quarters of the light beige marshmallow mixture to another piping bag (No. 2).

WHITE: Transfer one-quarter of the remaining marshmallow mixture directly to a piping bag. (No food coloring required.)

RED: To the remaining one-half of the marshmallow mixture, add 5 to 6 drops of red gel food coloring. Mix in the color with a spatula and transfer one-quarter to a piping bag (No. 1) and three-quarters to another piping bag (No. 2).

PIPE THE DESIGN

At some point, you will notice the marshmallow mixture has set. When this occurs, you'll need to soften it. To do this, just heat it in a microwave for 2- to 3-second intervals (it is important that you do not heat it in longer intervals). Between intervals, make sure to mix or use your hands to massage the mixture in the piping bags until it is soft. Be careful not to overheat it!

I. Line a baking sheet with parchment paper, cutting away any excess. Cover the parchment paper with a layer of cornstarch to a $^3/_8$-inch (1-cm) depth. Use a dough scraper to even out the cornstarch, so you have an even surface to work on.

(continued)

HOLLY JOLLY SANTA CLAUSES

(CONTINUED)

2. Cut a ½-inch (1.3-cm) opening at the tip of piping bag No. 2 of the red marshmallow mixture. Directly onto the cornstarch, pipe a ball shape about 1 inch (2.5 cm) in diameter to create the body. Make sure to pipe a small amount on the bottom two corners and blend it in, using a baking scriber. Make five Santa marshmallows at a time.

3. Then, cut a ½-inch (1.3-cm) opening at the tip of piping bag No. 2 of the light beige marshmallow mixture and pipe a ball shape on top to create the head.

4. Next, cut a scant ¼-inch (6-mm) opening at the tip of piping bag No. 1 of the red marshmallow mixture and pipe on Santa's arms and body (coat).

5. Cut a scant ¼-inch (6-mm) opening at the tip of the piping bag of the white marshmallow mixture and pipe the rim of Santa's hat and around his coat.

6. Use the same white piping bag to pipe on the beard, then pipe the mustache.

7. Cut a scant ¼-inch (6-mm) opening at the tip of the black marshmallow mixture and pipe on a belt and the shoes.

8. Cut scant ¼-inch (6-mm) opening at the tip of piping bag No. 1 of the light beige marshmallow and pipe the nose and hands of Santa.

9. Use the red marshmallow mixture (No. 1) and white marshmallow mixture to finish off Santa's hat.

10. Lastly, add the final details. Pipe a small amount of black marshmallow mixture onto your baking scriber and add two small dots to the face to create the eyes; do the same thing using the white marshmallow mixture to make a belt buckle.

11. Once you are done making all your Santa Claus marshmallows, carefully cover them with the remaining cornstarch on all sides, using a spoon and a clean, soft paintbrush to pat it in. Make sure they're fully covered and let them sit for 10 minutes.

12. Carefully brush off the excess cornstarch with a clean, soft paintbrush and transfer the marshmallows to a plate. Let them air-dry for about 2 hours before storing them in an airtight container.

BONUS

HOW TO MAKE A CHOCOLATE BOMB WITH MARSHMALLOWS INSIDE

Yield: 4 chocolate spheres

Hot chocolate bombs are chocolate spheres usually filled with cocoa mix and marshmallows. However, you can add your own twist to it by adding, for instance, instant coffee, caramels, instant chai latte or instant matcha latte. You can also add your own touch by decorating them with sprinkles, edible glitter or melted colored chocolate. The possibilities are endless!

There are two ways of using your chocolate bombs. Either you drop them into hot milk, or you pour hot milk over them. Both ways will do the trick. However, if you want to add the cute marshmallows you made, I suggest dropping the chocolate bomb into hot milk and letting them burst open slowly. I have noticed when pouring hot milk over my chocolate bombs, sometimes the marshmallows and certain details just melt away. After putting so much effort into making the marshmallows, you definitely want to showcase them!

INGREDIENTS AND TOOLS

200 g good-quality dark chocolate

4 tbsp (50 g) instant hot cocoa mix, divided

Sprinkles of choice

2 half-sphere silicone molds, 2½ inches (6.5 cm) in diameter

Pastry brush (optional)

1 cup (60 g) marshmallow designs of choice

Piping bag

HOW TO MAKE IT

1. First, melt the chocolate. You can either microwave it or use a double boiler. Microwaving works a lot faster but can also burn the chocolate easily, so you must keep a close eye on it. Using a double boiler will give you the most consistent melt but does take a lot longer.

MICROWAVE METHOD (USE LOWEST SETTING)

Break or cut the chocolate into smaller pieces and place in a microwave-safe bowl. Microwave in intervals of 30 seconds for the first minute and then in intervals of 15 seconds, mixing well after each interval. As soon as you notice 75 percent of the chocolate is melted, do not microwave it anymore; just keep stirring until the chocolate is completely melted.

DOUBLE BOILER METHOD

Fill a pot halfway with water. Bring it to a simmer over low heat and place a heatproof glass or stainless-steel bowl on top of the pot. Make sure the bottom of the bowl is not touching the water! The steam will be enough to melt the chocolate. Use a spatula to stir the chocolate until it is fully melted.

2. Take your silicone molds and add a little melted chocolate to each sphere. Use a pastry brush to brush the chocolate over the inside of the molds. If you do not have a pastry brush, a teaspoon will also do the trick. Just make sure the chocolate is distributed evenly.

3. Once the insides of the molds are all fully covered with chocolate, place the molds in the fridge to set for 10 minutes.

4. Repeat steps 2 and 3 to build up the chocolate layer. Don't worry about how the inside of the chocolate bombs look, just make sure that the entire chocolate layer is not too thin or else it might break when trying to remove the bombs from their mold. The chocolate should be almost 1/8 inch (3 mm) thick.

5. Once they are set, gently peel back the edges of the molds and carefully push out the chocolate spheres.

ASSEMBLE AND DECORATE

6. Heat a small skillet over the lowest heat and melt the edges of one of the chocolate spheres. This literally just takes seconds!

7. Fill the chocolate half-sphere with 1 tablespoon (12 g) of hot cocoa mix and a few marshmallows.

8. Take another chocolate half-sphere, melt the edges and place this on top of the chocolate half-sphere that contains the hot cocoa mix and marshmallows. Hold it for a few seconds to seal. Melting the edges of both chocolate half-spheres gives you an even surface to work with and makes the half-spheres stick better to each other, giving you the best-looking results.

9. To decorate the chocolate bombs, remelt the leftover chocolate by heating it in the microwave again at 15-second intervals or over a double boiler. Transfer to a piping bag and make a small cut at the tip. Drizzle the melted chocolate over the chocolate bombs and decorate with sprinkles of choice.

10. You can store your chocolate bombs in an airtight container at room temperature, in a dark and cool spot, for up to 2 weeks.

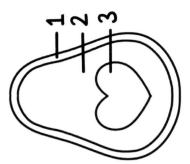
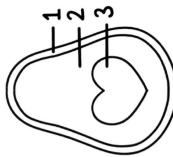

TEMPLATES

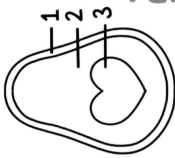
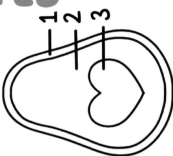

Lovely Avocado

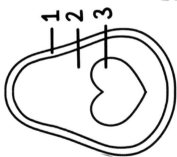
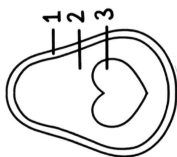

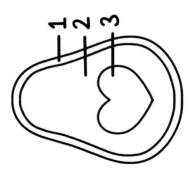
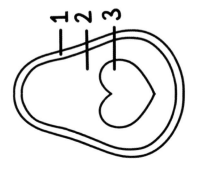

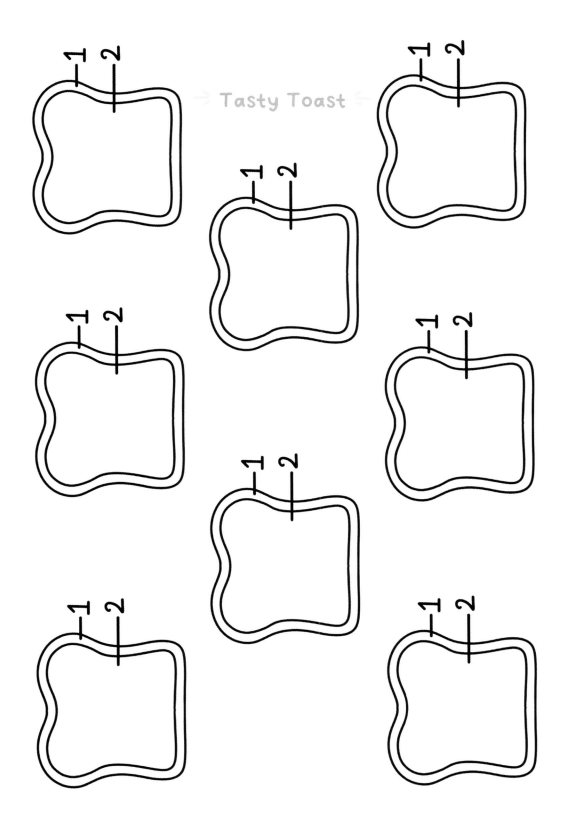

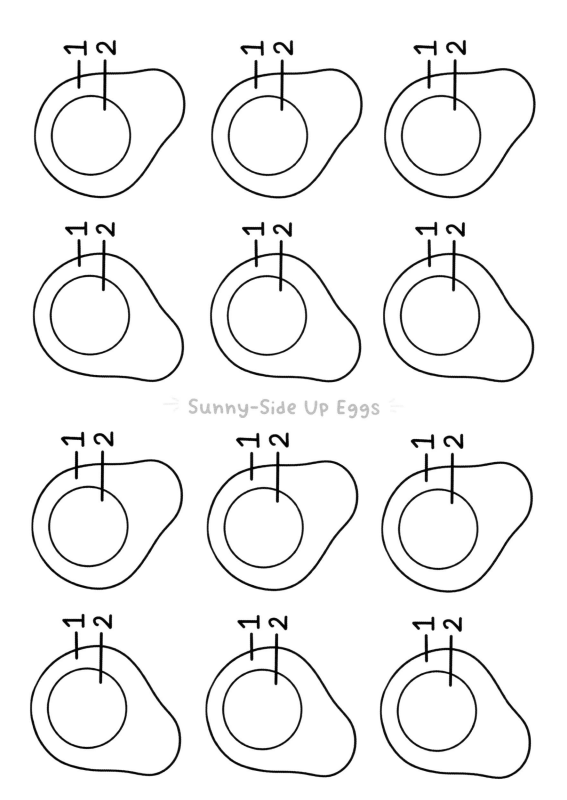

Sunny-Side Up Eggs

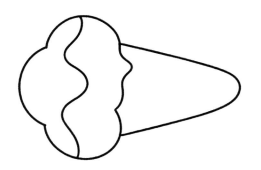
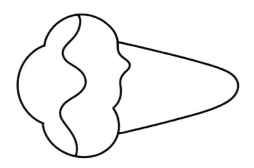

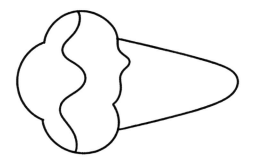
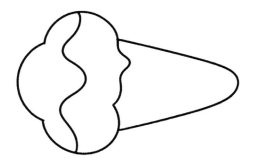
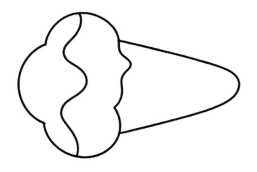
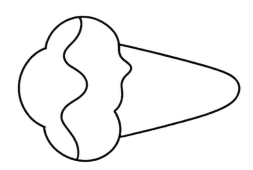
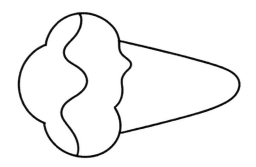
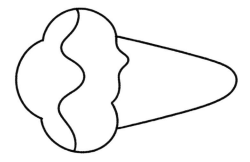

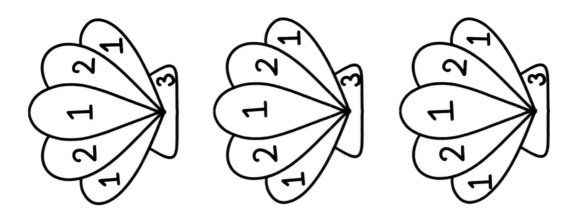

≈ Stunning Seashells ≈

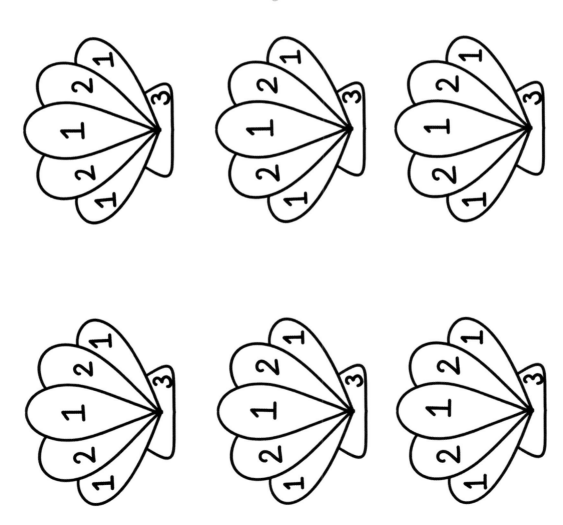

 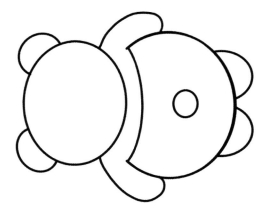

 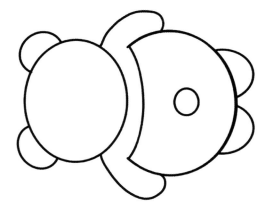

Colorful Unicorns

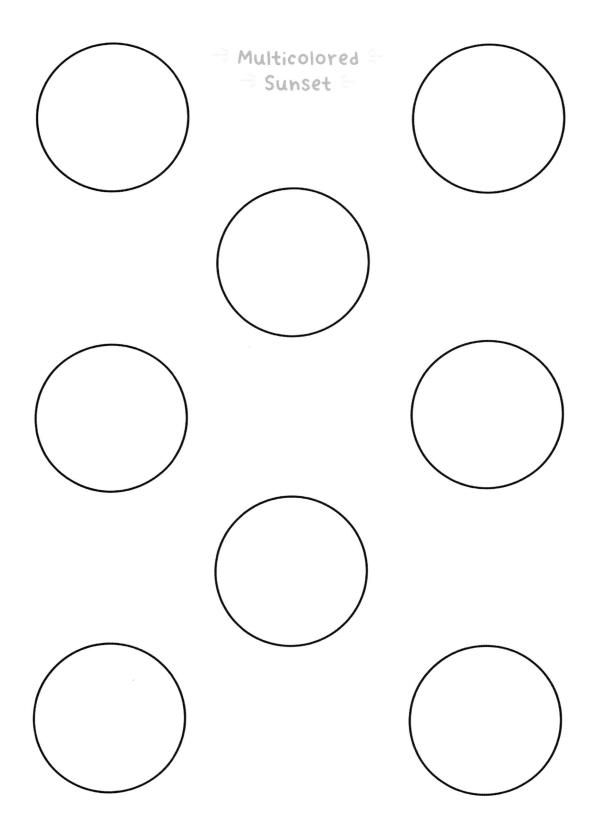

Multicolored Sunset

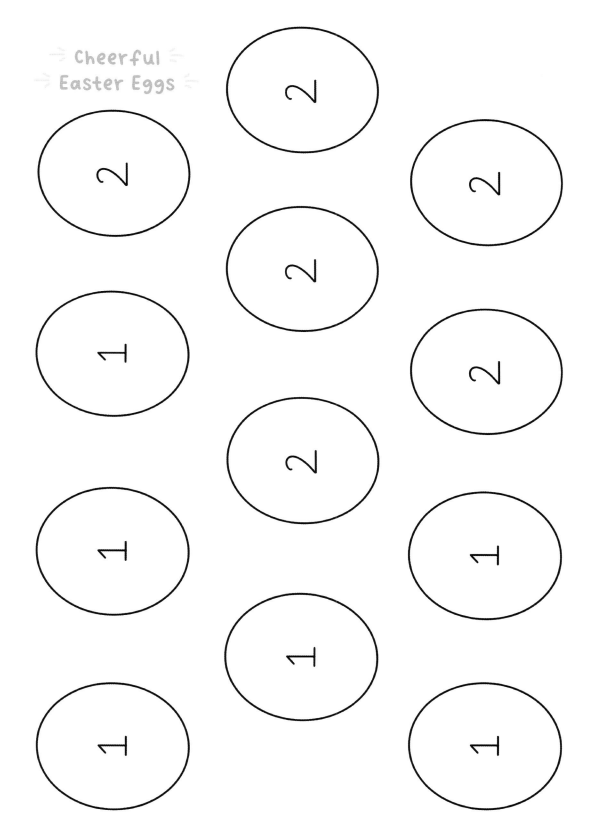

Cheerful Easter Eggs

Lovely Valentine Hearts

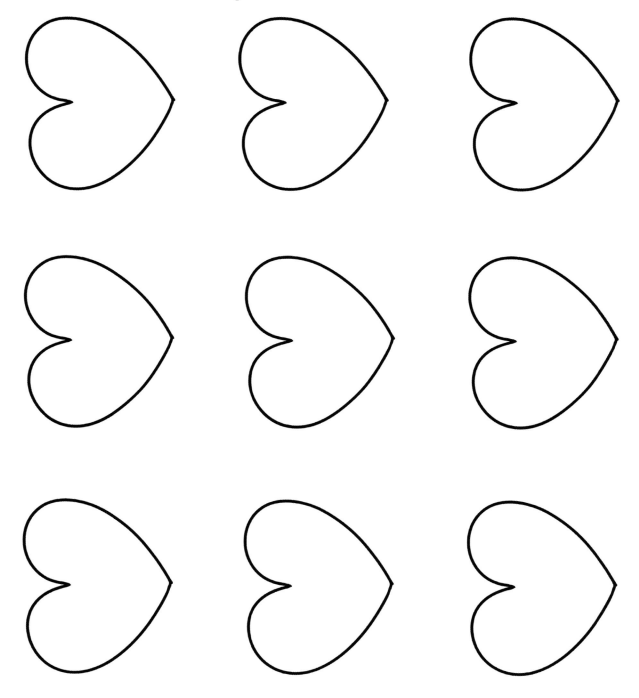

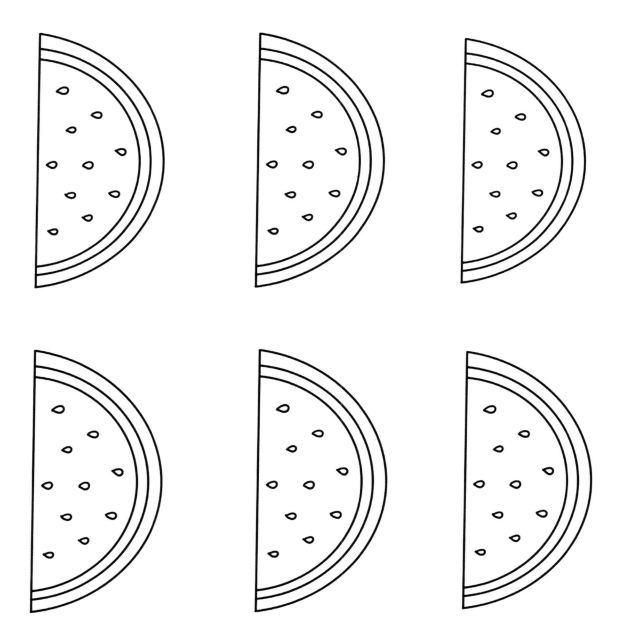

ACKNOWLEDGMENTS

This book would have not been possible without the people who have been following Cookingwithamyy/Amy's Kitchen on TikTok and Instagram since day one. Without their tremendous support and lovely messages, I would not have had the confidence to write this cookbook in the first place. It sounds cliché, but receiving messages from my followers about how my videos have brightened up their or their kids' day really drove me to write this cookbook and share my passion with others. So, now they can recreate these treats for themselves or for their loved ones. I'm truly thankful to each and every one of them.

I'm also extremely thankful to my sisters, Ai-hua Chao, Itsang Chao, I Chu Chao and Ai-yin Chao, who have always been great support and made me believe in my talent and dreams. Thank you for (taste) testing all my recipes and giving me your honest opinions. Not to mention my parents, Tse Yi and Cheng Hsiao Chao. Coming from an Asian family, I know Asian parents can have certain standards and expectations for their children, but thank you for allowing me to explore what I love to do and going after it.

I like to extend my gratitude to Wing Lun Fung, for taking the beautiful photos for this cookbook. You were amazing to work with and I am thankful for you showcasing my tiny creations in such a beautiful way.

Finally, I like to express my special thanks to Page Street Publishing, which gave me the opportunity to write this cookbook and for being an amazing help in guiding me throughout. Thank you for putting your trust in me.

ABOUT THE AUTHOR

Amy is a self-taught baker from the Netherlands. She created her popular cooking and baking social media accounts, Cookingwithamyy, in 2020. When the pandemic forced her to temporarily close her restaurant, she suddenly had a lot of free time on her hands. She had always enjoyed baking but never seemed to have enough time. With the forced downtime, she decided to pick it back up.

She first started her social media accounts just for fun and to share her recipes with her friends and relatives she unfortunately couldn't see due to the pandemic. However, beginning in 2021, one of her meringue cookie videos on TikTok went viral with millions of views. Her videos kept going viral worldwide and received much publicity.

She is now known for her adorable and unique character meringue cookies (floaties), marshmallows, macarons and many more items. She has been featured on several platforms worldwide, including PopSugar, Yahoo!, Food Network, Taiwan News, BuzzFeed, Nick Jr. and so on.

INDEX